THE COMPASS LEGACY

BY

José F. Nodar

Northport Booksellers/ Spring Farm NSW Australia

Copyright © 2025 by José F. Nodar

All rights reserved. No part of this publication may be reproduced, distributed, or transmitted in any form or by any means, including photocopying, recording, or other electronic or mechanical methods, without the prior written permission of the publisher, except in the case of brief quotations embodied in critical reviews and certain other non-commercial uses permitted by copyright law. Copyright of this publication is owned by José F. Nodar.

Publisher's Note: This is a work of fiction. Names, characters, places, and incidents are a product of the author's imagination. Locales and public names are sometimes used for atmospheric purposes. Any resemblance to actual people, living or dead, or to businesses, companies, events, institutions, or locales is completely coincidental.

Spring Farm NSW Australia/ José F. Nodar First Edition

ISBN 978-1-7637054-4-9 - Paperback

ISBN 978-1-7637054-5-6 - E-pub

ISBN 978-1-7637054-6-3 - Audiobook

Table of Contents

Chapter 1: The Revolution 2

Chapter 2: Francisco's Final Request 8

Chapter 3: Leaving Cuba 14

Chapter 4: Pineapple Pizza 19

Chapter 5: A Pact 23

Chapter 6: Dynamics 27

Chapter 7: La Brújula 32

Chapter 8: Family News 37

Chapter 9: Enough For Now 43

Chapter 10: Dead Serious 50

Chapter 11: The Beginning 57

Chapter 12: The Second Glow 64

Chapter 13: Couples Goals 68

Chapter 14: Dreams 72

Chapter 15: Sunday Morning 76

Chapter 16: Final Glow 79

Chapter 17: Miami 84

Chapter 18: Figuring It Out 90

Chapter 19: Steve's College Skill Set 96

Chapter 20: Flying to Cuba 103

Chapter 21: Mojitos 108

Chapter 22: Sightseeing 115

Chapter 23: Road To Baracoa 121

Chapter 24: Gran Cemí of Patana 126

Chapter 25: Connections 131

Chapter 26: Ramiro 136

Chapter 27: Coincidence 141

Chapter 28: Fake 146

Chapter 29: Treasure 151

Chapter 30: Secrets 155

About The Author: José F. Nodar 159

For
Rachel,
David,
And
Andrea.
You are always in my thoughts.

Chapter 1

The Revolution

The sounds of jubilant crowds were heard all around the streets of La Habana. Gunshots and cheers echoed from the open balconies as Fidel Castro's revolution celebrated its triumph. Cuban flags hung from the windows of homes and apartments. The smell of gun smoke permeated the air. The celebrations were loud and happy for most.

Inside Francisco Morales' home, the mood was anything but festive. Francisco sat slumped in a leather armchair, his once-powerful frame now frail and sunken with age. His wife, Elena, sat beside him, her hands wrapped around his, while their son Julio and daughter-in-law Camila sat across from them in a lounge. All were worried and the conversation between them was heated.

"We need to leave, Papá," Julio said urgently, standing up and starting to pace across the small room. "The revolution has already begun rounding up anyone who supported Batista, and even those who didn't. The old order is gone. We'll be next!"

Francisco wheezed and raised his hand, signalling for silence. His eyes, cloudy but still sharp with defiance, locked onto his son. "This is our home, Julio. We built our lives here—everything we have, everything we are. I won't let some young soldiers scare us away."

"It's not about being scared, Francisco," Camila said softly but firmly, stepping forward. "It's about survival. They've taken over La Habana. People are fleeing every day—bankers, merchants, even doctors. If we stay, what kind of life will we have here?"

Elena's lips tightened, her face a mask of silent worry. "Perhaps she's right, Francisco. The world is changing. What if they take the house? The shop? They'll take everything."

Francisco coughed into a handkerchief; his breathing laboured. "I've survived war, famine, dictators, and hurricanes. I am not leaving Cuba." His voice was ironclad, but it cracked at the edges, betraying his weakness.

"Papá, the revolution is not what everyone hoped for. There are rumours abound," Julio whispered, his frustration and fear sensed in his words. "If you won't leave for yourself, do it for the children."

Hiding and standing, in the dim hallway, Raquel, David, and Andrea crouched behind a half-open door as they eavesdropped on the adults. Raquel, the eldest at 13, leaned forward, straining to hear every word.

"Do you think we'll really leave?" David whispered to her; his brown eyes were wide with worry.

Raquel pressed a finger to her lips. "Shh. Listen."

Andrea, only 9 years old, curled beside her older siblings, clutching Raquel's dress. Her small face was tense with fear.

"Are we really going to leave Cuba?" David whispered, almost to himself. "Where would we even go?" again, whispering but this time to Raquel.

Raquel heard him, but she had no answers for her brother. They were as spellbound by the argument as they were frightened.

In the sitting room, the conversation escalated.

Julio clenched his fists, his frustration boiling over. "We can't stay here, Papá! It's not just about the house or the store—people are being arrested! Even executed! How much longer do you think until they come for us? A few days, a week, a month?"

Francisco gripped the armrest. His voice was like a low growl, and he was as stubborn as ever. "I will die in the same house where I was born, and my child was also born and raised. This damn revolution cannot force me out of my home!"

Suddenly, Francisco's eyes widened, and he clutched his chest, his face contorted in agony.

"Francisco!" Elena cried out, jumping to her feet.

"Papá!" Julio rushed to his side, catching his father just as the old man slumped forward, unconscious.

"Camila, call for help!" Julio shouted, lowering his father carefully to the floor. Elena knelt beside them, her hands fluttering uselessly as tears welled in her eyes.

"Francisco! No, no. Do not die on me today. Not today!" she screamed, her voice cracking.

Camila bolted toward the telephone in the corner, her hands shaking as she dialled the hospital.

Raquel, David, and Andrea huddled together in the hallway, frozen in fear.

"Is Abuelo going to die?" Andrea whispered, her voice small and trembling.

The three children huddled together, fearing something terrible was happening to their abuelo. "He'll be okay," Raquel whispered, though her own voice faltered with uncertainty.

David peeked through the gap in the door, watching as their father and grandmother desperately tried to revive Francisco.

"We have to do something," David whispered urgently. "We can't just stay here."

"What can we do? We are just children." Raquel shot back.

Andrea sniffled, burying her face in Raquel's side. Raquel held her tighter, trying to stay brave for both.

A brief time later, the ambulance arrived with a piercing wail that echoed through the streets of La Habana. The paramedics rushed inside, lifting Francisco onto a stretcher and wheeling him out to the waiting vehicle. Elena clutched her husband's hand, whispering prayers under her breath as the paramedics loaded him into the ambulance.

Julio turned back toward the house; his expression was grim. "Stay here with the children," he told Camila. "I'll go with Mamá."

"I will. I am sure he will be fine. I will let the niños know he'll be okay," Camila said, wiping tears away and looking at Julio for answers, but he had no answers to give.

The children watched from the doorway as the ambulance sped away into the night, its siren blaring.

Raquel, David, and Andrea stood in silence, still huddling together. The streets of La Habana were still alive with celebration, but inside the Morales home, it felt like their world was crumbling.

Chapter 2

Francisco's Final Request

The sounds of distant celebration still echoed through the streets on a second night. La Habana was alive with revolution, but in the Morales home, time felt as if it had stopped. A small lamp in Francisco's room cast a dim light across the faces of Raquel, David, and Andrea Morales as they were ushered in.

Their grandfather lay propped up on a stack of pillows, his breathing shallow and laboured. His skin was pale, and every movement seemed to drain what little strength remained. Around the bed hovered their grandmother Elena, their father Julio, and mother Camila; their faces drawn with grief and exhaustion.

"Come here, niños," Francisco motioning for them to come closer.

They approached the bedside cautiously, standing in a row like solemn soldiers. Francisco gave them a faint smile, the corners of his mouth twitching under his grey moustache.

"Don't look so scared, niños," he whispered. "I am dying. I had a good life, and I learnt a lot. But before I leave, there's one more thing I need to do." He reached beneath his blanket and pulled out a small, worn compass. The brass casing was dull, and the glass over its needle was scratched, hinting at many years of use. Yet, even in the dim light, it seemed to glow with a strange, quiet magic.

"Take this," he said, holding it out for Raquel to accept.

Raquel stared at the old compass in confusion. "What does it do, Abuelo?" she whispered, taking it delicately, as if it might break in her hands.

Francisco smiled, a glimmer of the adventurer he once was flashing in his eyes. "This compass," he whispered, "will take you to your greatest treasure. But it won't show you the way until you are each 25 years old. You must all be together for it to work."

David frowned, his brow furrowing. "Abuelo, what kind of treasure? Is it gold and silver?"

"No, this compass won't guide you to gold and silver, but it will give you what your heart desires most."

The children exchanged confused glances, unsure what to make of such a cryptic statement from their abuelo.

Sensing his strength was slipping away fast, Francisco continued. "The compass will guide you to the treasure only when all three of you are twenty-five years old. So, when little Andrea turns twenty-five, you'll get together, no matter where in the world you are, and follow the compass. Promise me you'll do this together."

A stunned Raquel nods and said: "I promise Abuelo," followed by David and even little Andrea whispered, "I promise, Abuelo."

Satisfied, Francisco smiled softly.

"Good," he murmured. "Now be patient, my little adventurers. Only a few years to wait for your treasure."

Francisco coughed.

Elena knelt beside him, clutching his hand tightly. Julio rested a hand on his father's shoulder, his jaw tight with unspoken emotion. As if he knew he was at the end, Francisco took one last breath, and as he exhaled, his face softened with peace.

That night, the family gathered in the sitting room. Grief was in their faces and their voices, but there was no time to mourn properly. Castro's revolution was tightening its grip on La Habana with each passing hour.

"We can't stay. We must leave," Julio said grimly, rubbing his face. "The revolutionaries are taking control of everything. People are being arrested just for being in the wrong place at the wrong time or saying the wrong thing."

"But this is our home. Francisco wanted us to stay."

Julio sighed heavily. "He didn't know what was coming. We must think of the children now. What kind of future will they have here?"

Camila, sitting quietly with her hands folded in her lap, finally spoke up. "If we leave, we can start over. We'll go to Miami, like so many others. It's the only way."

Elena sobbed quietly, torn between loyalty to her husband's memory and the fear of what might happen if they stayed. Finally, she said: "I am staying with my husband. In our home."

"No, Mami. You must come with us!" said Julio.

"No, mi hijo. At my age, I will just be a burden. I will stay and wait for your return."

Julio knew by his mother's face that she had made her decision and would not change her mind. The children sat huddled together on the floor, listening silently. Raquel clutched the compass to her chest, as if it held the answers to everything.

"Are we really going to leave Cuba?" Andrea asked.

"Yes," Raquel answered softly, wrapping her arm around her little sister.

In the next couple of days, Julio was able to get five tickets booked on the next Pan Am flight to Miami and on Wednesday before dawn, the family packed what few belongings they could carry. The streets were eerily quiet now; the celebrations giving way to a tense calm as the reality of the new regime settled over the city.

With tearful goodbyes to neighbours and friends, they made their way to the airport, where a plane waited to carry exiles away from the only home they had ever known.

As the plane took off, Raquel, David, and Andrea sat together holding hands, looking out the window, watching La Habana shrink into the distance.

Raquel slipped the compass from her pocket and opened it. The needle spun wildly, as if confused. Then it settled, pointing somewhere deep into the heart of the island they were leaving behind.

"It still points to Cuba," David whispered, staring at the needle.

"We'll come back one day," Raquel promised, her voice firm despite the lump in her throat. "When we're ready."

Andrea leaned her head on Raquel's shoulder, clutching her hand tightly. "Do you think the treasure will still be there?" she asked.

Raquel gave a small smile. "The real treasure is out there, waiting for us. It's something Abuelo wanted us to find when we're old enough to understand."

And so, as the plane carried them toward an uncertain future, the siblings made a silent vow: one day, they would follow the compass and discover what lay at the end of the journey their grandfather had set in motion.

Chapter 3

Leaving Cuba

Raquel, David, and Andrea sat together across the aisle from their parents. A stranger sat by the window, looking out. Their father tried to catch a glimmer of the vanishing coastline; his jaw clenched in silent grief. Their mother sat beside him, clutching a small bag to her chest as if the weight of its contents could anchor her in this storm of uncertainty.

Raquel, sitting in the middle seat, wrapped her arms around Andrea, who shivered more from fear than the cold, while on the aisle seat close enough for Camila to reach out if needed, David sat with his knees pulled up. His eyes were fixed on the outside, trying to swallow the knot of emotions swelling inside him.

The cramped cabin buzzed with low chatter and nervous whispers from other Cuban exiles, their faces pale with exhaustion. The engines roared as the aircraft cut through the sky; the sights of La Habana had long since faded into the clouds.

Camila and Julio leaned back in their seats across the aisle, both already calculating the new life they would need to build.

They had managed in a quick time to garner five tickets on the weekly Pan Am lights from La Habana to Miami. It had depleted their savings to almost nothing.

Julio's thoughts were of his mother.

Would he ever see her again?

She had stayed back, wanting to be there until the end of her life.

"What is a sixty-year-old woman to do in Miami," she had asked Julio.

With the constant humming of the plane, Julio fell asleep shortly after, thinking about his mother. The silence between the siblings was suffocating, each lost in their thoughts, until David broke it with a quiet question.

"Do you think we'll ever go back?"

Raquel turned her head, meeting her brother's gaze. "Someday," she whispered, though she wasn't sure if she believed it.

Andrea, sitting on Raquel's other side, hugged the compass tightly in her small hands. "Will it still work? Will the treasure wait for us?" she asked in a voice barely louder than a breath.

Raquel gave a small, reassuring smile, though her heart felt heavy. "It must. Abuelo wouldn't have given it to us if it wasn't real."

David nodded, though uncertainty lingered in his expression. "What if we never find it? What if we forget how to follow it?"

Camila overheard and leaned from her seat and whispered: "You won't forget, and when the time is right, the compass will show you the way. You'll understand when you're older."

The hum of the plane's engines filled the silence between them as they fell quiet again. Raquel looked down at the compass in Andrea's hands, watching the needle spin lazily before settling in a direction that felt impossible to follow now—back toward Cuba.

Suddenly, a flight attendant came around, serving breakfast. A little tray containing lunch and started helping the children with their trays. All three looked at the tray and simultaneously said: "¿Qué es esto?"

The flight attendant spoke Spanish and answered, "Es su almuerzo."

Their lunch was something strange. It included mashed and candied yam in a hollowed out half an orange, a slice of turkey, dressing, and gravy with a generous sized hot roll and a large pat of butter. And a slice of pecan pie for dessert. The children did not know, but they had just been presented with their first Thanksgiving lunch.

They gobbled down their food and, still hungry, both David and Andrea asked Raquel for more. Raquel, who had studied "Inglés" in school, knew she would ask for more, but she couldn't remember the right words. Undeterred, she raised her hand and the flight attendant return and asked what she needed.

Raquel simply said in her best English: "Repeat, repeat."

The flight attendant giggled and said: "Lo siento. No más," and picked up all the trays, leaving the children wondering if food was also going to be hard to find in Miami.

The plane touched down with a soft thud on the runway in Miami. The cabin shuddered, and the Morales family exchanged weary glances as the flight attendants announced their arrival. This was it—home, for now.

"Welcome to Miami, folks," the pilot said over the intercom, his voice cheerful, though it brought little comfort. "Local time is 12:15 a.m. We hope you enjoy your stay."

Julio let out a slow breath, rubbing his temples. "Enjoy," he muttered under his breath, the word feeling bitter on his tongue.

The family stood and gathered their meagre belongings. A few bags, a couple of heirlooms tucked carefully away—and the compass, of course, resting in Andrea's small hands like a fragile promise. They shuffled down the aisle and into the jet bridge, joining the throng of other Cuban exiles stepping into a strange and new world.

As they exited the terminal into the humid Miami air, Raquel gave one last glance over her shoulder, as if she could still see the shores of Cuba somewhere behind them.

She whispered to herself, "One day, we'll go back. We must."

Her siblings followed silently, and the Morales family crossed into an uncertain future.

The compass—and the hope of finding what it promised—carried close to their hearts.

Chapter 4

Pineapple Pizza

Raquel watched the ceiling fan as it spun lazily. It did nothing to cool the suffocating two-bedroom apartment. Sitting at the table doing her homework, she watched her mother cooking a soup. She heard the front door open and in walked in her father dragging his feet home after his second shift, smelling of grease and sweat from working as a busboy. Raquel knew her mother wasn't that dissimilar; exhausted from cleaning houses five times the size of their cramped apartment, and yet, there now cooking for her family.

Raquel sat at the small kitchen table, which doubled as a homework station and a dinner table, flipping through David and Andrea's school assignments. Andrea pouted, her hair tangled from the humidity, her Spanish-language workbook a mess of wrong answers.

"I don't understand anything!" Andrea whines, pushing the book away.

"Me neither," David grumbled from the corner.

Raquel's eyes flicked toward her father. Julio sat heavily on the sagging couch, head in his hands, muttering something about needing a third job. Camila stood at the stove stirring a pot of soup, her silence cementing any complaint she could utter and simply stated: "Julio, a third job? There are not enough hours in the day. You need your rest."

Julio reacted to David and Andrea and almost screams: "What's wrong with these kids? They need to learn English. They must. How can they make it in this country if they can't even finish their schoolwork?"

"Julio, por favor, don't yell at the children. They are trying," Camila warned. "They're trying," she mumbles to herself.

Raquel was silent and just bit her lip. She was doing her bit to help with her siblings. She had taken the role of translator, problem-solver, and, at times, part-time parent without complaint, but she also felt the pressures and cracks were starting to show. Her siblings were slipping behind in school, and the weight of everything was weighing on her.

"It's not our fault," David shot back defensively. "People talk too fast. And half the words don't even make sense!"

"English is a stupid language," Andrea declared in agreement with her brother. "Why do they say 'read' and 'read' the same way, but mean different things?"

Julio groaned. "Why does everything have to be so hard in this country? Camila, maybe we made a mistake coming here?"

Camila did not answer Julio, and silence filled the room.

Everyone felt the dream of a better life was like a distant mirage. Would they survive? Or would they have to return to Cuba? Even then, would the communist government take them back?

Camila continued to stir the pot slowly, her eyes just looking at the pot as if in a daze. David and Andrea sniffled, on the verge of tears.

Raquel hated seeing her family like this: broken and so far from the lively, loving household they used to be.

And then, out of nowhere, she thought of something and just blurted it out. "You know… at least no one's telling us to eat pineapple pizza."

For a moment, they all stopped what they were doing and looked at Raquel.

Then Camila shook with suppressed laughter. David let out a loud snort, and even Julio, weary as he was, cracked a smile.

"Yes, yes, the one with pineapple! How can anyone call that a pizza?" Andrea shrieked and giggled uncontrollably.

"Oh God, you are right, Andrea. How can they call that a pizza?" David adds, doubling over in laughter.

Julio leaned back into the couch, chuckling himself. "Pineapple on pizza. These American people are crazy."

Camila continued stirring the soup with one hand while the other clutched her stomach. "It's true! What is that? Pizza should be simple, not a science experiment."

Raquel smiled. Her statement fixed nothing. Their struggles were still there, but here, for now, they were laughing together about the absurdity of life in exile.

At least at this moment, thought Raquel, this is enough.

Chapter 5

A Pact

The new apartment smelled like fresh paint and hope. It was larger—much larger—than the old two-bedroom, with a real dining room and a balcony overlooking a busy street. The noise of car horns and distant music from passing trucks drifted up, but it didn't bother the family. After a year of struggle, this apartment felt like proof things were getting better.

Raquel stood at the threshold of the shared living room, looking out at David and Andrea. David, now twelve, was sprawled on the couch with a library book, finally at ease with English. Andrea, who had just turned ten, sat at the small desk in the corner, colouring, her tangled hair tamed into a loose braid.

The familiar frustration and helplessness of last year had faded. The siblings no longer needed Raquel to translate every word, and though the memory of their struggles still lingered, their resilience had transformed them.

"Come here," Raquel said, motioning them over. Her voice had grown more confident. She wore her excitement like armour—high school was on the horizon, and for the first time in a long time, she felt ready.

David put down his book, and Andrea abandoned her crayons, joining their sister on the floor. Raquel pulled the compass from her pocket, its brass edges worn smooth from years of handling. Raquel placed the compass between them. "It's time we make a pact," she said.

Andrea blinked, curious. "A pact?"

"Yeah," Raquel said. "We've been through a lot. We've had to grow up fast. But I think we need to make sure that, no matter what, we stick together—no matter how far life takes us."

David sat up straighter. "Stick together… How?"

Raquel smiled. "We'll meet again when Andrea turns 25."

Andrea's eyes went wide. "That's forever from now!"

"It'll go faster than you think," Raquel said, grinning. "We'll all be adults by then, with different lives, maybe even living in different cities in the USA. But wherever we are, we come back together. And we use this—" she pointed at the compass, "—to follow wherever it leads us, just like Abuelo wanted."

David rubbed his chin like an old man pretending to think. "And what if it leads us somewhere weird, like a swamp?"

Raquel rolled her eyes, but Andrea giggled.

"Then we go," Raquel said. "Because it's not just about where we go—it's about keeping the promise. To him and to each other."

David and Andrea exchanged glances, the weight of the moment settling in. It wasn't just a game. It was a commitment—a reminder that, no matter what the world threw at them, they would find their way back to each other.

"So, what do you say?" Raquel asked, holding out her hand.

David smirked. "Fine. But only if you promise not to boss us around in the future."

Raquel laughed. "Deal."

Andrea placed her small hand on top of Raquel's. "Okay, I'm in too. But we must meet. Even if we're super old."

"Twenty-five's not old," Raquel said, squeezing Andrea's hand.

David added his hand to the stack. "It'll be an adventure."

Raquel nodded, her heart swelling. "It already is."

They sat in silence for a moment, each feeling the significance of their pact. In this strange, sprawling city, far from the world they once knew, they had made a promise—to their abuelo, to each other, and to themselves.

Julio's voice called from the kitchen, "¡Niños! Dinner's ready!"

Camila chimed in from behind him teasingly; "And don't make me say it twice!"

The three siblings stood up; hands still joined for one last squeeze. The weight of exile had lessened, and with it, new possibilities had emerged. Their family was healing. Their dreams were starting to feel reachable again.

As they headed toward the dining room, Raquel slipped the compass back into her pocket. She knew it would guide them someday—when the time was right.

But for now, it was enough to know they had each other. And that was the only compass they needed.

Chapter 6

Dynamics

The soft hum of the washing machine in the background blended with the lazy weekend atmosphere as Raquel, David, and Andrea sat around the dining table. Sunlight streamed through the large window, casting warm patterns across the hardwood floor. Raquel leaned back in her chair, stretching her arms.

"Alright," she said, brushing a lock of her dark hair behind her ear. "It's time we talk again."

David looked up from his phone, his brows knitting. He already knew what was coming. Andrea fidgetted with her camera, adjusting the lens out of habit, her mind half-focused on the moment, half-drifting toward her latest photo project.

Raquel tapped the table to get their full attention. "I'm leaving in a couple of months."

Andrea's face clouded for a second before she hid it, focusing again on the camera in her hands. "We know, Raquel. You're off to New York University. You got the scholarship. We've heard it, like, fifty times."

Raquel gave her a soft smile. "Yeah, but I need to remind you both—because things are going to change. I won't be around every day, and... you'll have to step up."

David sank deeper into his chair, crossing his arms. "I get it. I know."

"You do?" Raquel asks, raising an eyebrow. "Because it's not just about you and school. It's about helping around the house too, supporting Mom and Dad, and... well, Andrea."

David shifted uncomfortably. He could feel the weight Raquel was placing on him, and it was not lost on him that with her gone; the dynamics in the home were going to shift. "I'm already helping."

"David, I know," Raquel said, softening her tone. "But it's not just chores. It's about being there. You want to be an engineer, right? That's going to take focus. And if you want to make it happen, you'll need to start now."

David sighed but nodded. He knew she was right. He'd been dreaming of building things since he was little, and Raquel leaving felt like a reminder that his future was coming at him fast.

Andrea cleared her throat, breaking the tension. "I don't need babysitting, you know."

Raquel smiled. "I know you don't. You're almost fourteen, practically a grown-up."

Andrea grinned, finally looking up from her camera. "I am a grown-up. And I know what I want to do. I'm going to be a photographer."

"I know you will," Raquel said warmly. "And you're going to be amazing at it. But you'll still need your brother."

Andrea wrinkled her nose in mock protest but didn't deny it. There was a bond between them, unspoken but strong, and she knew she relied on David more than she let on.

Raquel leaned forward; her voice soft but firm. "Here's the thing. No matter where we are—whether I'm in New York, or you're off somewhere figuring out your dreams—we stick together. Always."

Andrea's eyes flickered with something unspoken, a hint of fear about the future and what it might look like without Raquel at home. "Even if we're far away?"

"Even then," Raquel said. "When Andrea turns twenty-five, we're having a reunion. No matter where we are, we get together. It's non-negotiable."

David smirked. "To discuss the compass, right?"

Raquel grinned. "Yes. To see what the compass is all about and see what Abuelo meant. And if you think about it, twenty-five—it's not that far off. You'll see."

Andrea rolled her eyes but smiled. "Fine. Twenty-five. Deal."

David shrugged. "Deal. But when you come back for that reunion, you'd better be ready to hear about all the cool engineering stuff I'll have done by then."

Raquel chuckled. "And I'll want to see Andrea's photography exhibition too."

Andrea raised her camera with a playful smirk. "Oh, don't worry. I'll be famous by then."

Raquel reached across the table, placing a hand on each of their shoulders. "We've got a lot ahead of us. But no matter what, we've got each other. Always."

For a moment, the three of them sat in comfortable silence, the noise of the world outside feeling far away. Though their paths were starting to diverge, they knew that some bonds, like family, only grew stronger. And no matter where life would take them, Raquel's promise would hold them together.

David glanced at Raquel, the weight of responsibility settling a little more firmly on his shoulders—but also a new sense of purpose.

Andrea adjusted her grip on her camera, already imagining all the pictures she'd take, both of her siblings and the adventures to come.

"Twenty-five," Raquel whispered to herself, as if it's not just a promise, but a future waiting to unfold.

The soft hum of the washing machine stopped and beeped three times, alerting them load was done.

"Come on guys, let's go and hang up the clothes and surprise Mum when she returns from work and have them all dried, ironed, folded and put away," Raquel said.

"That is a lot of work," Andrea said, but placed her camera on the table and headed to the laundry, realising she was going to be helping her mother more when Raquel left for college.

David hesitated for a moment but thought to himself: "I better learn how to do laundry if I am also going to go to engineer university," and followed Andrea.

Smiling, Raquel felt David and Andrea would do fine when she left.

Chapter 7

La Brújula

Raquel sat on the edge of her bed, her desk lamp providing the only glow in the room. With her window part open she heard the familiar sounds of New York City buzzing; the city that never slept. She shivered a little and closed the window. The cold reminded her that winter was coming. Returning to her bed, she wrapped herself in her favourite throw blanket, the one her mother sent her from Miami, and pressed the phone to her ear as it rang.

"Hola, mija!" Camila's warm voice filled the line as she recognised the phone from the caller id.

Hearing her mother's voice always grounded and reminded her of the many conversations they'd had at the family's kitchen table back home.

"Hi, Mamá," Raquel said, "How's everyone? How are you?"

"Oh, we're good! Can you believe he got a full scholarship to Georgia Tech? Your brother is going to be an engineer!"

Raquel smiled, picturing David hunched over his desk, his head deep into his books, scribbling equations. "Yeah, I heard. I'm proud of him. He's grown these past few years. "

"Yes, mija. And Andrea is working part time at that photography studio downtown, Crown Photos—the one near the art district, you remember? And she's already talking about colleges. She wants to be close to you, so she's looking at the Rochester Institute of Technology."

Raquel chuckled. "RIT? Does she know that's seven hours from New York City?"

"Not yet," Camila said, also laughing. "You know how your sister is. Once she gets something in her head, she runs with it."

Raquel grinned, imagining Andrea with her camera slung over her shoulder, explaining how photos need to be taken while staying "close" to her big sister.

"How's Papá? And the restaurant?"

"Oh, Papá is doing very well managing the restaurant, thank God. The restaurant is thriving, and…" Camila paused, "we're thinking about opening our own place."

"What? Seriously?"

"Yes! We've been brainstorming names, playing with ideas. We're finally ready, I think. We've worked hard enough—it's time to do it for ourselves."

"Mamá," Raquel said, "I've been thinking a lot lately. About... Cuba. And our roots."

"Tell me, mija. What's on your heart?"

Raquel shifted on the bed, pulling the blanket tighter. "I've been learning so much—about literature, about history. But I keep feeling this pull, this... need to understand where we came from. I want to know the truth about our family, our roots in Cuba. It's hard to explain. I just feel like I need to rediscover that part of me. But at the same time..."

"You feel caught between two different worlds," Camila finished gently.

"Yeah. Like, I love being here, in New York City, studying what I love. But there's always this part of me that feels, I don't know, incomplete. I guess it might be nostalgia for a place I left so long ago as a young child."

Camila's voice was soft and understanding. "That's a heavy thing to carry, Raquelita. It's normal to feel that way. Cuba is part of who we are, whether or not we've lived there. It's in the stories, the food, the music... it's in us."

Raquel rubbed her eyes, suddenly overwhelmed. "It's hard, Mamá. I don't know how to balance it. I live here now. I am building a life but also wanting to connect with what we left behind."

"I know, mija. But remember, you don't have to figure it all out now. Take it slow and one day at a time. You're doing what you want now and getting ready for your future: studying, learning, growing. And you'll find your way to the answers in time. Just don't forget, you're not alone. We're always here, and our roots will always be a part of you."

"Thanks, Mamá. I needed to hear that."

"Of course, mi amor, and don't you worry. You will succeed, graduate and we'll be waiting for you. We'll all be together soon."

Raquel was quiet, thinking over what her mother has just said.

"Soon, Mamá. After graduation."

"Oh! One more thing, Raquel. We've come up with a name for the restaurant."

Intrigued, Raquel chuckled. "What is it?"

"Well, we have narrowed it down to two names. One: La Cocinita 1898, and the second one is La Brújula," Camila said proudly.

Raquel's heart skipped a beat. "La Brújula and the other choice is Cocinita 1898?" She thought for a moment but had to ask: "What does the 1898 refer to?"

"1898 is the year of the independence of Cuba from the Spanish," answered Camila.

"I see. Mamá, if I were to get a vote, I would go for something from our personal past. I like La Brújula."

Camila took a moment to ponder Raquel's suggestion before saying: "Yes, because no matter where life takes us, we always find our way back to what matters. Your Abuelo would agree with that. We will go with La Brújula. I am sure your father will agree. This way we honour his father as well."

Raquel's chest tightened, the meaning behind the name hitting her deep. "I love it," she whispered.

"We will as well," Camila replied. "Now you just focus on school, okay?"

"Okay, Mamá. I will."

They exchanged a few more words with Raquel promising to call again soon, before they finally said their goodbyes.

Hanging up, Raquel stared at the phone in her hand and took a deep breath.

She'd be home soon.

Chapter 8

Family News

Even though it was winter, the Georgia sun beat down on David's car as he loaded the last of his bags into the trunk. The student apartment in Midtown was mostly cleared out—just a mattress, a few stray books, and the remnants of fast-food wrappers left behind from long nights of studying. He told the landlord how much to remove it from the premises and since he got a fair price, told the landlord to take it out of his deposit and to post him the balance to his parent's place in Miami.

His semester at Georgia Tech was finally over. After two and a half years of relentless coursework and going year-round to graduate, the pressure had lifted, but only slightly. A new job with McDonald Professional Services Inc. waited for him, starting in six weeks, and David was running on borrowed time.

He slammed the trunk shut and sighed, taking in the moment. He hadn't seen his parents or his sisters in what felt like forever. Each visit home since he'd left for college had been short, awkward, and dominated by the guilt he carried—guilt for not calling enough, for studying instead of spending time with them, and for abandoning some of Raquel's responsibilities when she'd first left for college, leaving them to his mother to take on. Now Raquel had graduated, and Andrea was on a break from school. His parents had asked him to come home for this rare window when they'd all be together.

David tapped the steering wheel nervously, the engine humming beneath him as he began the long drive down I-75 to Miami. His heart felt heavy. Family time was supposed to be relaxing, but he knew there were unresolved tensions—conversations that never happened and memories they never shared.

Would they resent his absence? Would Andrea give him grief for locking himself away with textbooks during his visits? He tried to shove those thoughts down and focus on the week ahead: seven days at home, a few awkward conversations to survive, and then back to Georgia to hunt for an apartment near his new office in Kennesaw.

David pulled into his parents' driveway in Miami. It was late afternoon, and Camila stood by the window and saw as David drove up. She rushed outside, arms wide open, and pulled him into a tight hug. Julio followed behind, clapping David on the back with a grin that softened some of David's unease.

Inside, Raquel was already sitting at the dining table, scrolling through her phone, and gave him a quick wave without looking up. Andrea was sprawled across the couch, a mischievous glint in her eye. She looked more confident than the last time David saw her.

"Hey, big brother, you decided to show up this time?" teased Andrea.

Raquel cut in with a playful grin. "Don't let him off the hook that easy. He'll probably lock himself in his room for the next seven days."

David grinned. "Not this time. I've got an entire week, and no textbooks."

They all laughed, and for the first time in a while, David felt a small weight lift off his chest.

That evening, over a sprawling dinner, Andrea dropped her bombshell. "So, I've decided," she said casually, setting her fork down. "I'm leaving school."

"Andrea..." Camila started; her voice edged with concern.

Andrea held up a hand. "Before you say anything, I got a job offer. It's with The Global Nomad, the travel magazine? I start in three weeks, and the pay is exceptionally good. Like... fantastic."

"But you're quitting college? Two years in? What about finishing your degree?" Julio frowned.

"It's a once-in-a-lifetime opportunity, Papi."

Julio leaned back, crossing his arms. "How much are they paying you?"

Andrea pulled out a small notepad and wrote the amount. She slid it across the table to Camila, who read it, eyes widening, and then she passed the note to Julio, whose eyebrows shot up in disbelief.

"That's a lot. You got a contract or something? You got this in writing?" Julio asked, still trying to process the number. Andrea nodded with a big grin on her face.

Julio placed the note in his pocket, looked straight at Andrea and added: "But if this doesn't work out, you can always come back and help at the restaurant."

The comment stung a lot, but Andrea knew her father meant well, but she had decided. She hoped he would understand her choice better later.

Camila clapped her hands together. "Enough talk! There's more food. David, Raquel, come help me set the table for dessert. I made your favourites."

With that, the mood lightened, and the family enjoyed the desserts their mother made; flan and Dulce tres leche. David watched as his sisters teased each other over who had to help clean up, and for a moment, everything felt right.

After dessert and everyone was enjoying a Cuban café, the conversation had shifted to lighter topics and Julio interrupted. "Children, we have an announcement to make." He waited for them to look at him before continuing. "The restaurant is doing really well; so well that I—we—are thinking about opening another one in Tampa."

"We were thinking of calling it La Brújula #2," Camila added with a grin.

The siblings groaned in unison.

"Seriously, mamá, that's the best you could come up with?" asked Raquel.

Andrea shook her head, suppressing a laugh. "How about something with a little more... flair?"

In a furious conversation, suggestions were thrown out and discussions happened on the various names, but to no success. There was no agreement, until David suggested one that made them all pause and nod in agreement.

"How about you name it Sabor de La Habana?" he suggested.

"'The flavour of Habana' in English," added Andrea.

Even Julio looked impressed.

"You know," Camila said thoughtfully, "I think that name could work."

Julio nodded. "I like it. Maybe you kids know what you're doing after all."

As the night wound down and they said their goodnights, heading to their old bedrooms, David felt a strange sense of peace.

The week ahead might not be perfect, but for now, after sitting at the dinner table surrounded by laughter and love, he knew everything was going to be okay.

Chapter 9

Enough For Now

David returned to Atlanta to get ready for his graduation and start his new job. A week later, his parents and siblings showed up for it.

Now the graduation ceremony was a blur.

Caps were thrown into the air, faces beamed with pride, and the weight of years of hard work culminated in a single, fleeting moment.

David should have felt something more. Relief, perhaps. Or satisfaction. Instead, he just felt hollow.

When his parents and siblings came to the graduation, everyone was happy. He had done what he wanted to do.

Three months later, after the family had gone their separate ways once more, and David was well into his new job, he sat alone in his apartment. His diploma framed and leaning against the wall; he stood and went to the window, staring out. The Atlanta skyline glittered in the night, a maze of lights that mirrored his chaotic thoughts.

"I did everything right," he told himself. "Followed the plan. Good grades. The engineering degree. A solid job at a reputable firm. What more could anyone ask for?"

But deep down, he knew the answer. He wanted more. And yet, he couldn't define what more meant.

The compass sat in his desk drawer, buried under a pile of unopened mail and scattered receipts. Raquel had passed it on to him while she was overseas for a month and didn't want to lose it.

He hadn't looked at it in years, not even when she'd handed it to him. Not since Raquel's insistence on their pact; not since that cramped Miami apartment where they dreamed of the future as kids. The memory of their laughter and promises made his chest tighten.

"It's childish," he thought. "A stupid relic from a past I don't have time to dwell on."

But the compass still haunted him, even when he tried to ignore it. Its presence was like a ghost, a reminder of the family history they'd never fully understood. What had Abuelo mean about "following where it leads"? Why had he given it to them, of all things, before they left Cuba?

David shook his head, frustrated. "I can't waste my time chasing ghosts. Raquel and Andrea can play with fantasies if they want but I have a life to build."

That was the truth. Or at least, the truth he told himself. Yet the life he was building felt like a cage. His job paid well, and his colleagues respected him, but the endless meetings and calculations felt meaningless. The work kept his hands busy, but his heart… Empty.

And then there was the guilt. The unspoken weight he carried as the middle sibling—the quiet one who was supposed to bring balance. Raquel was always the leader, Andrea the dreamer, but David? He was the one who had to hold everything steady. Even now, he felt the pull of responsibility. For their family. For their shared past.

But what about me? The thought startled him, almost as if he wasn't allowed to have it. What about what I want?

He had distanced himself from them: Raquel, who had her own plans, and Andrea, who was still searching for hers. The calls came less frequently now, their voices tinged with disappointment when he rushed them off the phone. He hated the way it felt, like a slow unravelling of something once unbreakable. But he didn't know how to fix it, or if he even wanted to.

"If I don't focus on my career now, what's the point of everything we sacrificed?"

He tried to believe it, but the logic rang hollow. The truth was, he didn't know what he was working toward anymore. The dreams that once felt so urgent—the big house, the shiny car, the respect—had lost their lustre. He wondered if they were ever really his dreams, or if he'd borrowed them from the world around him.

David sighed, running a hand through his hair. He glanced at the desk drawer, his fingers itching to pull it open, to take out the compass and see if it still pointed north.

But he didn't move. He was afraid of what it might mean if he did.

What if it leads Raquel, Andrea, and me somewhere I can't come back from?

The thought terrified him. And yet, somewhere deep inside, it also thrilled him.

Shaking his head, David turned away from the window and flicked off the light. The city outside continued to shine, indifferent to his doubts and burdens.

As he lay in bed that night, staring at the ceiling, he was about to close his eyes when the phone rang. David looked at the name, smiled and just thought of one word before answering: "Excellent."

"Hello?"

"Hey, David! It's Lisa."

"Oh, hey, Lisa. What's up?"

"You sound thrilled to hear from me," she said with a slight laugh.

David smirked a bit and answered: "It's not that. Just... didn't expect a call this late."

"Well, I didn't expect to still be thinking about that ridiculous meeting we had today. But here I am. Anyway, I was about to head over to Piedmont Bar by the park, and I thought you might want to join me. You know, unwind a little?"

David paused before answering. "Uh... I don't know, Lisa. It's been a long day, and I was kind of planning to—"

"Come on, David. Don't make me beg. It's Friday. You can't just sit at home all night pretending you care about your Netflix queue."

He chuckled. "I don't pretend. I do care."

"I'll buy the first round."

"Lisa, listen…"

But before he finished the sentence Lisa used a mocking voice and added: "Please? Pretty please? Just one drink. If you're miserable, I'll let you leave. No hard feelings."

"You're relentless, you know that?"

Lisa laughed. "I'll take that as a yes."

"Fine. I'll meet you there in twenty."

"Great! I'll grab us a good spot. Don't flake on me!"

"Yeah, yeah. See you soon."

David hung up, got off the bed, and walked to his closet.

As David pulled a shirt from the hanger, his thoughts began to drift. The desk drawer flashed in his mind. The damn compass, buried under the clutter. It'd be so easy to say it was lost. During the move, it could've been tossed in a box and disappeared, just like a dozen other things he hadn't bothered to unpack. Raquel would believe him, probably. Or maybe she wouldn't, but she'd let it go, eventually.

He pulled the shirt over his head, catching his reflection in the mirror. But even as he laced up his shoes and grabbed his keys, he knew the truth: he wasn't going to tell her. The compass wasn't lost. It never would be. He'd held on to it for this long for a reason, even if he couldn't explain why.

As he shut the door behind him, locking the apartment and heading out into the cool night air, the weight in his chest didn't feel any lighter. But it didn't feel heavier either.

Lisa's laughter would distract him for a little while. And maybe that was enough for now.

Chapter 10

Dead Serious

Andrea slid her camera bag from her shoulder onto the table, exhausted but exhilarated from her latest assignment in Patagonia. She'd landed at LAX an hour ago, but traffic had been terrible, so the usual normal ride took longer, and since she hadn't Uber-ed it from the airport, the taxi ride had been quite expensive. She headed into her bedroom, dropped the suitcase on the bed, and immediately went to the bathroom.

Turning on the tub water, she went to the fridge and got a bottle of cold wine, not even paying attention to the label. Taking her clothes off and tossing them on the floor, she slipped into the hot water and settled in. She needed to wash the trip off her skin.

It had been another glorious trip; very successful.

People were excited when she emailed the photos. Now all she wanted was a few moments of peace before having to go back to work the next day.

Andrea felt hungry, and she figured she probably had some type of microwave food in the freezer which will do for tonight.

Finishing in the tub, she dried herself wrapped a towel around her hair and her robe around her waist and walked into the lounge area. These she sat with her bottle of wine, almost gone, and a glass in her hand as she perused the surrounding walls. They were all decorated with prints of her work. Misty mountaintops, bustling cityscapes, and her favourite: candid portraits of people from every corner of the world. Her job kept her moving, searching for new vistas, but there was one thing that always seemed to tether her to the past: the compass.

Is it magic? Or is it just a piece of metal carrying the weight of Abuelo's dreams? She wondered, as she often did.

Her phone buzzed, interrupted her thoughts.

"Andrea! Finally, got a hold of you. You're back in town?"

"Just landed yesterday. What's up, Bill?"

"I wanted to see if you had time for dinner. I want to catch up, hear about all the amazing places you've been. Maybe you can even make me feel better. I was stuck here editing videos in a stuffy office while you were off gallivanting around Patagonia."

Andrea did not feel like going out, but Bill was her favourite coworker and besides, anything was better than a frozen TV dinner. "How about some tacos, Bill? You up for it?"

"Tacos, sure, yes, I am. What do you suggest?"

Andrea did not take long to come up with a suggestion: "You know the spot on Hollywood with the salsa that burns your mouth with every bite, the Mexican Goal Bar on West 4th Street? If you do, then meet me there in an hour."

"You're on," and they both hang up at the same time.

Andrea gulped down the last of the wine, punched a number into the phone asking for an Uber and scheduling it for thirty minutes before hurrying back into the bathroom to dry her hair. Quickly she threw on some jeans, a light yellow top, a pair of flat shoes and grabbed her purse and camera. Before she left, she made sure to tuck her passport in a plastic bag and place it under her potted Kentia palm—the only green thing inside her apartment, and hurried downstairs.

She arrived at the sports bar early. The different smells emanating from the kitchen every time a server went into the kitchen, but the aroma of fresh tortillas and grilled meat dominated the air. Since she didn't have a booking, she was seated towards the rear of the place.

Bill showed up minutes later, all smiles, and they dove right into her latest trip while Bill relayed all the most recent office gossip.

The food came alone with some horchata. Andrea, even with her Cuban background, had never had or heard of horchata until Bill introduced it to her. It was a sweet drink, and while originally from Spain it was quite popular in many Spanish-speaking countries. Horchata was made with rice, cinnamon sticks, and water. The rice was blended, then the ingredients were soaked overnight. After the rice and cinnamon were discarded, the remaining liquid was then flavoured with vanilla, sugar, and ground cinnamon. It was quite yummy, and Andrea felt prey to this drink from her first try.

After the tacos were gone and the second round of horchata arrived, Bill leaned back in his chair, looking at Andrea. "So, you're always on the move, always chasing the next adventure. But you seem... I don't know, like there's something else driving you. Something more than just a love for photography."

Andrea hesitated, her fingers tracing the rim of her glass. She'd never shared the story of the compass with anyone outside her family, but there was something disarming about Bill's curiosity.

"There is something, Bill. But you must promise not to laugh, okay?"

With a big grin, Bill said: "Cross my heart."

Andrea pulled a photo of the compass from her bag, setting it carefully on the table between them.

"This compass belonged to my abuelo. He gave it to my siblings and me before we left Cuba. He told us to follow it, that it would lead us to something important. Something magical. I have kept this photo with me all the time."

Bill's eyebrows rose.

"Where is the compass now?"

Taking a quick sip, Andrea continued. "Well, my older sister had it until a few weeks ago when she left for Europe and gave it to my brother, David, to keep. He's in Atlanta now." Andrea finished her horchata with a satisfied sigh. "My siblings and I agreed as kids when I turn 25, we're going to follow it. Together. Wherever it leads us."

"Wait one minute. What do you mean 'it leads you'? Like it pulls you instead of pointing its arrow? I don't understand," asked a surprised Bill.

"Yes, Bill, I realise it sounds so bizarre. How can a compass not point north, right? Maybe the darn thing is broken, and that's why it's not pointing north. It is crazy. But this compass has always pointed somewhere different every time my siblings or I hold it. Not north like a normal compass."

Looking sceptical, Bill asked: "And you really believe it's magical, Andrea? You sure your grandfather wasn't pulling your legs?"

Andrea met his gaze steadily. "No, Bill. He gave it to Raquel right before he passed away. I don't just believe it. I know it."

Bill let out a low whistle, leaning forward to study the compass. After another moment of intense study, he stood up. "I am going to get us a couple of beers. I think I saw they have Cabotella Mexican Ale. You want one?"

Andrea nodded and watched Bill go to the counter. She wondered if she did the right thing in sharing the photo with him, but before she can regret it, returned saying, "That's one hell of a story. But come on, Andrea—magic? Treasure? Really? It sounds like something out of a fairy tale."

Andrea's expression cooled, though her voice remained calm. "Maybe it is. But fairy tales have truth in them too. You don't have to believe me, Bill. Just wait. When I turn 25, I'll tell you what we find."

Sitting back, Bill looked at Andrea. "You're really serious about this."

"Dead serious," Andrea answered with a grin.

The conversation shifted after that, back to lighter topics, but Andrea couldn't help feeling the weight of what she'd shared. Bill had seemed stunned, even a little doubtful, but Andrea didn't need his belief. She had enough of her own to carry her through.

As they said goodbye, Andrea felt a flicker of anticipation rise in her chest, and no matter where the compass led them to in the future, she knew it would change everything.

Chapter 11

The Beginning

Raquel sat in the centre of the bar. Most of the office had come to celebrate her birthday and while they attempted a rendition of "Happy birthday," too much wine and beer had crossed their lips.

The past year had been good for her: a successful return from Europe, a promotion at work, and now, a stronger connection with David after her stop in Atlanta. He had seemed happier, more grounded. He had even mentioned someone named Lisa, though he didn't go into much detail. Raquel suspected Lisa had something to do with the lightness in his voice.

"Speech!" someone called out, and Raquel rolled her eyes.

"Speech? No chance! You all just want me to embarrass myself and tell you all to slack off tomorrow."

The table erupted in laughter, and Raquel took a sip of her drink, revelling in the moment. But as the chatter continued, she excused herself to the restroom, leaving behind the boisterous celebration.

Raquel leaned over the sink, washing her hands as the warm water ran over her fingers. She reached for her purse on the counter, but as she lifted it, something slipped out—a small metallic object that hit the counter with a soft clink.

The compass.

Raquel stood alone in the bathroom, staring at the compass. The brass casing, usually dull, was glowing faintly, just barely, but she could see it glowing enough to make her heart race. The needle, which normally just wandered aimlessly, pointed decisively south.

Southeast. Toward David.

She grabbed the compass, the glow fading as quickly as it had appeared. She mumbled to herself, "Did I see that, or did I imagine it? Was it real and what does it mean?"

Without a second thought, she tucked the compass back into her purse and hurried out of the restroom to return to her table.

Her excitement was hard to contain sitting at the table. Raquel clutched her purse securely. Beatriz Holmes, Raquel's manager and a sharp observer, tilted her head, narrowing her eyes at Raquel.

"Hey, birthday girl. What has gotten you so jumpy?" Beatriz asked, a teasing edge in her voice.

"Nothing. Nothing really, Beatriz," Raquel said quickly.

Beatriz looked at Raquel and said: "Uh-huh. Sure. You are glowing more than those sparklers on your cake earlier."

Raquel tried to laugh it off, but Beatriz's gaze dropped to her purse, still clutched in Raquel's hands.

"What's that small bulge in your purse?" Beatriz asked, pointing.

"Just an old keepsake," Raquel said casually, though her fingers tightened around the strap.

Beatriz leaned in, curious. "Oh, come on, let me see! Is it some kind of antique?"

Raquel hesitated, then relented, pulling out the compass but keeping her grip firm on it. "It is just a... family heirloom. Nothing special."

Beatriz tilted her head, studying the compass. "Looks cool. Vintage. What does it do?"

Raquel shrugged, trying to play it off. "Not much. It just sits in a drawer most of the time."

Beatriz grinned. "Looks like it is worth more than just sitting in a drawer. You sure there's not some secret treasure map inside or something?"

Raquel forced a laugh, quickly slipping the compass back into her purse. "If there is, it is lost on me. Anyway, enough about that. Let us get back to celebrating, yes?"

Beatriz eyed her suspiciously, but let it go. Raquel, however, could not shake the urgency in her chest.

Raquel rushed into her apartment, dropping her purse on the couch and flipping open her laptop. She logged onto Skype, her fingers trembling slightly as she clicked on the group call with David and Andrea.

David appeared first, his apartment dimly lit. "What's up, Raquel? Kind of late, isn't it?"

Andrea's face popped up next, her backdrop a mix of travel posters and framed photos. "Raquel, you look… frazzled. Did you drink too much at your party?"

Raquel ignored the teasing. "Guys, listen to me. Something happened. With the compass."

Both siblings straightened slightly, their casual demeanour shifting.

Andrea squinted. "What do you mean? Did it... do something?"

Raquel held up the compass to the camera. "It glowed. I'm not kidding. It glowed. And it pointed south. Towards you, David."

David frowned. "Glowed? Compasses do not glow Raquel. Are you sure it wasn't a trick of the light or something?"

"I know what I saw, David," Raquel said firmly. "I don't know how or why, but it's never done anything like this before."

Andrea leaned closer to her screen; her expression was serious. "Do you think... do you think it's trying to tell us something? Or lead us somewhere?"

Raquel nodded. "I don't know, but I feel like we can't just ignore it."

David sighed, rubbing his temples. "Raquel, I get it. But come on. It's a compass. Maybe it's old wiring or... I don't know, some weird reaction to the environment."

Andrea shook her head. "It's not just a compass, David. You know it's not. Abuelo said it was special."

Raquel looked between them. "We made a pact, remember? To follow it when Andrea turns 25. That's not far off now. I think... This is a sign. We must take this seriously."

David hesitated; his face conflicted. "I'm not saying I don't believe you. But... I've got work, and Lisa, and things are finally settling down for me. I can't just drop everything for this."

Andrea frowned but nodded slowly in agreement with her brother. "I get the urgency, Raquel. I want to figure it out too, but honestly, I don't know what to make of it either. Maybe we just wait and see if it happens again. I mean, after all, Abuelo said, when all of us are 25, the compass will lead us on its magic trip. I have a bit to go yet to reach 25, so we can just wait, right?"

"That is correct, Andrea," interjected David, then he paused. "Wait, I got an idea," said David. "How about you FedEx me the compass tomorrow and I'll watch it? If it glows when I have, it means something. If it does not, then I keep it until I reach 25 in two years. How's that for an idea?"

Raquel sighed, her frustration bubbling beneath the surface. "Fine. But don't just brush this off, okay? Promise me you'll think about it."

They both nodded, though their expressions remained uncertain.

Andrea chimed in, "And, if it glows again, then you send it to me, David, and I will what it does. Like I said, I have ways to go until I turn 25," she said, twirling her right index finger in the air giggling.

As the call ended, Raquel closed her laptop, holding the compass tightly in her hands. She didn't know what it all meant, but she was sure of one thing: this was only the beginning.

Chapter 12
The Second Glow

A couple of years passed, and the three siblings almost forgot about the compass because of their busy lives.

Raquel returned from Africa after cementing another deal.

Andrea was in California increasing her worth as an influential and sought-after photographer.

David had now achieved a new title as senior development engineer with his firm and had become involved deeper with Lisa, who left the company for another firm to avoid any impropriety.

David and Lisa were lying in bed after a night out celebrating his 25th birthday and Lisa woke up to a glow emanating from his nightstand. Shaken, she woke up David.

David saw the glow, opened the drawer, and found the compass glowing and pointing not south but west. It dawned on him that the compass wanted to be with Andrea.

Lisa and David got up and turned on the computer to Skype with both Raquel and Andrea, letting them know what had happened.

The solution, after a few moments of discussion, was simple. Get the compass to Andrea.

"It makes sense," David said as he and Lisa finished the conversation and promised to send the compass to Andrea in the morning.

On her side of the country, Raquel sipped her coffee, the steam curling up lazily as she tilted her head to one side, watching Andrea through the screen. It was just the two of them now. "Well, I guess we've got more than the compass to talk about," she said, a knowing smirk playing on her lips. "David and Lisa seem... serious."

Andrea leaned back in her chair, her camera shaking slightly as she adjusted her laptop on a cluttered desk. She ran a hand through her hair, brushing away the stray curls framing her face.

"Yeah," she said, her tone thoughtful. "It's kind of surreal, isn't it? I mean, David. Serious about someone?"

"Right?" Raquel laughed softly, taking another sip. "I remember when we used to joke, he'd marry his job before anyone else."

Andrea chuckled. "Lisa's good for him, though. She's grounded, but she's not afraid to call him out when he's being... you know, David."

"True." Raquel's voice softened. "It's nice to see him happy. But let's be real: do you think he's ready for something big? Like, ring-big?"

Andrea's eyes widened slightly, and she shook her head with a laugh. "You're jumping ahead! They've been together for what, two years? I mean, yeah, Lisa left the company for him, and they've got this whole... synergy thing going. But marriage?"

Raquel shrugged, setting her mug down. "Maybe I'm projecting. You know how Mom keeps dropping not-so-subtle hints about all of us settling down."

Andrea rolled her eyes. "Oh, don't remind me. Last time we talked, she asked if I was 'mentoring any cute young photographers.'" She made air quotes and a dramatic face that made Raquel burst into laughter.

The glow of their sibling banter faded slightly as Raquel leaned closer to her screen, her expression more serious now. "But really, Andrea. This compass. It started with me. It found David, and now it's coming to you. Do you think this is just some family heirloom mystery, or is it... something more?"

Andrea frowned, her fingers tapping idly on the desk. "I don't know. But it's strange that it's pointing west now. And the glow... it's almost like it's alive. Do you think it's leading us somewhere? Like we're supposed to do something with it?"

Raquel nodded slowly. "Maybe. Or maybe it's just been waiting for the right time. The three of us have been so focused on our lives—Africa, California, engineering—we haven't exactly had time for... whatever this is."

Andrea sighed, glancing at the small suitcase she'd already started packing. "Well, it looks like I'm about to find out. When the compass gets here, I'll let you both know what happens. But Raquel... if this thing turns into some kind of wild treasure hunt or destiny-fulfilling quest, you better be ready to hop on a plane."

Raquel grinned. "Always. You know me. I can never resist a delightful adventure."

"Or drama," Andrea teased.

As they both laughed, the glow of the compass seemed to linger in the back of their minds; a quiet reminder their story was far from over.

Chapter 13

Couples Goals

Andrea was halfway through closing her laptop when the familiar Skype chime sounded again. She raised an eyebrow and clicked to answer. And again, Raquel's face appeared.

"What now, sis? Can't sleep," Andrea teased.

Raquel shook her head with a smirk. "Nope. I called because we need to talk about something far more interesting. David and Lisa."

Andrea groaned and flopped back in her chair, a playful grin tugging at her lips. "Of course. The relationship analyst strikes again."

"Come on!" Raquel leaned closer to her screen. "Am I the only one who finds it hilarious that our brother, the self-proclaimed workaholic, is suddenly a romantic? Letting Lisa in on the compass conversation? That's serious business."

Andrea laughed, her head tilting back. "Oh, I know! I couldn't believe it either. I mean, David barely let us into his life for years, and now he's all 'Hey Lisa, let's discuss this family heirloom that glows mysteriously.'"

Raquel's grin widened. "Right? And can we talk about how he's handling his first real relationship? At his age? It's like watching a teenage rom-com, except it's starring our 25-year-old brother."

Andrea snorted. "Do you think he's reading relationship advice blogs or something? Like, 'Top Ten Tips for Dating When Your Comfort Zone Is a Spreadsheet.'"

"Guaranteed," Raquel replied, laughing. "But seriously, though, Lisa seems great. I'm just wondering how Mom's going to react. You know she's going to grill him the second she meets Lisa."

Andrea groaned dramatically, throwing her hands in the air. "Oh, you just know she's going to hit Lisa with, 'So, when are you giving me grandchildren?' at least three minutes into the conversation."

"And don't forget the passive-aggressive comments about how David 'waited so long' to find someone," Raquel added with a wicked smile, "he just turned 25, for goodness' sake."

"Poor Lisa." Andrea shook her head. "She has no idea what she's walking into."

Raquel chuckled softly, her laughter fading into a warm smile. "Joking aside, it's kind of nice, isn't it? Seeing him... happy. He's always been so focused on his career. I think Lisa balances him out."

Andrea nodded. "Yeah, it's weird, but good. He deserves it, you know? Even if it's a little awkward watching him try to figure it all out."

The sisters shared a moment of fond silence before Andrea glanced at the clock. "It's getting late for you, isn't it? Don't you have an early morning?"

Raquel groaned. "Ugh, yes. But this was worth it. Promise me you'll call when the compass arrives?"

Andrea held up her hand in a mock salute. "Scout's honour. If anything happens, you'll be the first to know."

"Good. And if it tries to drag you on a wild adventure, call me immediately. I need a reason to use my frequent flyer miles."

Andrea laughed. "Deal. Goodnight, Raquel."

"Goodnight, Andrea. And seriously, keep an eye on David. If he starts talking about 'couple goals,' we need an intervention."

Andrea grinned as the call ended, the laughter still lingering as she shut down her laptop. Despite the uncertainty surrounding the compass, she felt a sense of comfort in her siblings' banter. Whatever lay ahead, they would face it together. Even if David's love life became a subplot in their family saga.

Chapter 14

Dreams

Over the next few years, the compass became a distant memory, tucked away in Andrea's nightstand. Life unfolded in its unpredictable, messy, and sometimes magical way.

Andrea met Mark at a trivia night at the neighbourhood pub. His encyclopaedic knowledge of 90s sitcoms and his hopeless inability to remember movie quotes somehow charmed her. Within a year, they both left their own apartments and were renting a larger, cosier apartment together, complete with mismatched furniture—and Mark's overly friendly cat, Whiskers.

Meanwhile, Raquel dove deeper into her art, finally landing her first solo gallery show. It was a tremendous success, though she still wrestled with that nagging feeling of never being "good enough." She found solace in her friends, in bursts of creativity at odd hours, Mark, and his humour and attention to her and, of course, in sporadic texts from Andrea and David.

David, now ever more the grounded sibling, had embraced his engagement to Lisa with gusto. Their wedding planning was nothing short of a Herculean effort, but David approached it with the precision of a man assembling a 1,000-piece puzzle. Lisa adored his methodical approach until he suggested colour coding the guest seating chart.

Then, late one summer evening, Andrea was cleaning out her nightstand. Mark had made a casual comment about how they seemed to have "ten thousand junk drawers," and Andrea intended to prove him wrong.

She pulled out old receipts, pens that had long since dried up, and a single mismatched sock. At the very back, nestled between an unused notebook and a dusty paperback, she found the compass. It looked the same as ever, though its light had remained dormant since it flicked off the day it arrived.

Andrea hesitated, her fingers hovering over it. Something about the compass felt heavier now—not in weight but in presence, as though it had been waiting. Curious, she picked it up, half-expecting it to spark or glow.

Nothing.

"Still just a weird little trinket," she muttered, though her voice held a tinge of doubt.

As she moved to set it aside, her phone buzzed with a text message from Raquel: "Hey sis, I had a dream about that dumb compass again last night. Weird, huh? Call me."

Andrea stared at the message, then at the compass. A faint flicker of light pulsed from its centre—brief, almost imperceptible, but unmistakable.

Her heart thudded. She reached for her phone and dialled Raquel.

"Okay, this is getting creepy," Andrea said as soon as Raquel picked up. "The compass just... did something."

Raquel's sharp inhale echoed through the line. "You're kidding. I was just about to tell you about my dream."

Andrea's hand tightened around the compass. "What kind of dream?"

"The kind that makes you wonder if we're still in the real world," Raquel replied. "And it wasn't just me. David texted me earlier—he said Lisa's been seeing strange symbols in her sleep. He thinks it's nothing, but I think... maybe it's connected."

Andrea felt the compass grow warm in her palm. "I think it's time we figure out what this thing actually is. My birthday is in three days. We need to have some preliminary plans if it does something... big."

"Big? What do you mean by big, Andrea?"

"I don't know, sis. Something. Blow all the lights in LA? Cause for lighting to appear! Something big."

Raquel's voice steadied. "Agreed. Let's talk to David and Lisa. We need to sort this out."

The compass pulsed again, stronger this time, as though it had been listening all along.

Chapter 15

Sunday Morning

Julio sat up, running a hand through his damp hair. The dream had been so vivid, so real; it felt like he had just left another world and stepped back into this one. Camila propped herself up on one elbow, her brow furrowed as she watched him, and he related his dream.

"What do you mean you sensed Francisco?" she asked, her voice still tinged with sleep but laced with curiosity.

Julio sighed, swinging his legs over the side of the bed. "It wasn't just sensing him. He was there, standing in front of me, clear as day. He didn't speak, but his eyes... they said everything. I felt it in my chest, Camila. He wanted me to know something."

Camila sat up fully now, concern etched on her face. "And the children? You said they'd be coming home after Andrea's birthday. What did they look like? Were they okay?"

"They were okay," Julio said softly, reassuringly. "But they were different. Older, wiser, like they'd been through something big. Raquel had a calmness about her, like she finally understood her purpose. David looked... determined. Focused. And Andrea..." He trailed off, shaking his head. "Andrea was glowing, literally glowing, like she was carrying something—power, maybe, or knowledge—I don't know. They all had this weight about them, but it wasn't a burden. It was like they'd been chosen for something."

Camila reached for his hand. "And Francisco? What was his role in all of this?"

Julio closed his eyes, trying to recapture the feeling from the dream. "It felt like he was guiding them. Like he'd been watching over them all this time, preparing them for something. He didn't say a word, but the look in his eyes told me everything. They have something to do, something that will change everything. And they'll come home with news. Big news."

Camila squeezed his hand, her voice steady despite the unease that was beginning to settle in her chest. "News about what?"

"I don't know," Julio admitted. "But it's tied to that damn compass my father gave Raquel right before he passed away. I know it is. That thing—it's not just an heirloom, Camila. It's something more. And somehow, Francisco and the children are connected to it."

Camila bit her lip, thinking, but before she could speak, Julio shook his head. "No. We wait. They have their own journey to complete, their own choices to make. If Francisco is involved, they'll find their way. But we need to be ready. When they come home, everything will change. For them, and for us."

Camila leaned against him, the weight of his words sinking in. "Do you think they are ready?"

Julio walked to her side of the bed and inched his way beside her, staring out the window as the Miami sun rose, painting the sky in hues of gold and pink. "We'll have to be. Whatever this is, it's bigger than us. We just must trust that they'll find their way to whatever it is they're meant to do."

Outside, the world continued as usual, oblivious to the quiet storm brewing in their lives. But for Julio and Camila, Sunday morning would never feel the same again.

Chapter 16

Final Glow

A bright glow woke them up at 5 AM, enveloping their entire bedroom and surprising them. It was the compass.

Andrea picked it up from her nightstand as Mark roused beside her. The glow was already subsiding a bit. Andrea sat up on the bed, the compass still warm in her hands. Its needle continued to first point north, then south and then west and then again south and continued to repeat the sequence, repeatedly, its glow dimming each repeat of the sequence.

Mark rubbed his eyes, his voice groggy but tinged with concern. "What the hell was that, Andrea?"

Andrea nodded, her mind racing. "Yes, but it's not just glowing. It's… guiding me." She looked at him, her voice steady despite the adrenaline surging through her. "It's pointing south, well, sort of. It's repeating a sequence. Look!"

She showed him the compass and he nodded blearily. "Indeed, it is. What do you think it means?"

"I think it's telling me to go to Miami. To tell Raquel and David to meet me there."

Mark blinked, the absurdity of the situation sinking in, but he knew better than to doubt her. "Okay, let's take a breath. Why Miami? Why now?"

Andrea hesitated, clutching the compass. "I don't know how I know, but I do. It's not just about me. It's about all three of us, maybe even Mom and Dad, too. Something's going to happen, Mark, and we need to be together for it."

Mark rubbed the back of his neck, glancing at the clock. "It's your birthday, Andrea. I was planning a surprise party."

Andrea cut him off gently, placing a hand on his arm. "I'm sorry, Mark. I appreciate the party, I really do. But this is bigger than a birthday. I can feel it. Please, trust me on this."

He studied her face for a moment, seeing the determination there. With a resigned sigh, he nodded. "Okay. We'll do this. But we need to act fast."

Andrea looked at the time and immediately grabbed her phone and dialled Raquel. It took a few rings before her sister answered, her voice groggy. "Andrea? It's eight in the morning. Happy birthday, but this better be—"

"Raquel," Andrea interrupted. "Listen to me. I need you to come to Miami. Not for my birthday. I will call David to do the same. We need to meet at Mom and Dad's house in three days."

Raquel was silent for a moment, her voice cautious when she spoke. "Andrea, what's going on?"

"I don't have time to explain everything, but it's about the compass," Andrea said, gripping the glowing object tighter. "It's glowing again, and it's pointing south, well sort off. It is continuing a sequence. First north to you, then south to David, then west to me, and finally south again. I believe that means Miami. Then it repeats it over and over again. The glow is still there but dimming. I am not sure how long it will last. I know it sounds crazy, but trust me, okay? You need to come. Take sick leave, use vacation days, whatever it takes We need to be there in three days."

"Why three days, sis?"

"I don't know but just be there in three days. I'll also call our parents, so they're not surprised when we all come down."

Raquel's hesitation was palpable, but eventually, she sighed. "Fine. I'll call David. I will meet you in Miami in three days."

"Thank you," Andrea said, relief flooding her voice. "I'll text you my flight details and get David to do the same when I speak to him."

Next, Andrea dialled David and went over the same conversation with him. David did not hesitate and told her he and Lisa would be there in three days as well.

Taking a big breath, Andrea called her parents. Julio answered after one ring; his tone sharp with concern. "Andrea? Is everything okay?"

"Dad, I need you and Mom to prepare for all of us to come home. Raquel, David, and I—well, everyone as Mark and Lisa will be coming too. We need to meet in Miami in three days. It's about the compass."

Julio's silence was told. Finally, he said, "We'll be ready."

Andrea sensed her father knew something but did not ask.

Julio, feeling that Andrea was waiting for something from him, simply said: "I'll explain what I can when you're all here."

After hanging up, Andrea turned to Mark, who was already packing a bag.

"We'll call the airline after breakfast. You told them three days, so we have time to wrap it up in the office and get a reasonable fare, even on such short notice," he said. "If this is happening, we might as well get there well prepared."

Andrea hugged him, grateful for his support. "Thank you. I know this isn't what you planned for today."

Mark chuckled softly, kissing the top of her head. "Hey, what's life without a little unpredictability? Besides, if anyone can figure this out, it's you."

As they prepared to have an early breakfast and head out to the office, Andrea kept the compass close, its faint glow a constant reminder that this was only the beginning. Something monumental thing was on the horizon, and it was pulling her and her family toward it, like a tide that couldn't be resisted.

Chapter 17

Miami

The three siblings and their partners arrived at Miami airport almost at the same time since Andrea had made sure that they all shared their details to make it easier for them to get to their parents' house. Andrea hired a minibus for the occasion.

As they all gathered in the baggage claim area, David and Andrea spotted Raquel and a man holding her hand, and they looked at each other.

"Well. Wonder who that is with Raquel," said David.

"I don't know, but we will find out before we get to our parent's home. Lisa, Mark, do you mind getting our bags? We need to speak with Raquel and, well, her man. I am not sure what to call him."

Both Lisa and Mark smiled and just nodded, looking for all the bags.

Walking up to Raquel, Andrea gave her a quick embrace and said, "Good to see you, sis. Who do we have here?"

Looking a bit embarrassed, Raquel was about to speak when the stranger spoke first: "Hello you must be Andrea and her friend, Mark, correct? My name is Steve Fitzpatrick. I believe I have been Raquel's love interest, at least for the last three years. I am sure she has not said a word to anyone about me, correct?"

Raquel's jaw dropped. Nothing was coming out of her mouth but suddenly Andrea and David burst out laughing and even Steve joined in as Mark and Lisa came up to them with all the bags.

"What is so funny, Andrea?" asked Mark.

"I think we need to head to the pickup station and wait for the minibus. It should be here in thirty minutes."

"Thirty minutes? It should have been here waiting for us, Andrea. Did you not tell them the time?" quipped David.

"In case one or all of us ran late because of flight issues, I booked it for thirty minutes later. Besides, this gives Raquel time to tell us all about Steve before Mum and Dad grill her."

Again, more laughter at Andrea's statement.

As they waited for the minibus to arrive, Raquel went through the story of how Steve and she met, connected, and had been living together for the last three years, all without telling any of them.

This brought a lot more smiles and laughs.

"Well, I can't wait to see their reaction, sis," said David.

"I don't know why you are so worried about your parents. They are hip, girl, you know that?" said Lisa.

Before Raquel could answered, the minibus pulled up and a young, good-looking Hispanic man called out: "Are you the Morales?"

"We are indeed. Let's go guys," answered Andrea as they each gave the driver their bags and jumped inside.

Once on their way, they chitchatted about how much the city had changed since they'd left. Raquel whispered a few things to Steve, who just nodded and smiled a lot.

As the minibus pulled into the driveway of Julio and Camila's home, the three siblings and their partners stepped out, stretching their legs, and taking in the familiar sight of the house they'd grown up in. The warm Miami air was heavy with the scent of hibiscus and the distant hum of the city.

The front door opened, and Julio and Camila stepped out onto the porch, their faces lighting up with joy.

"Finally, my children are home!" Camila exclaimed; her arms wide open as she made her way to greet them.

Julio was close behind, his gaze scanning the group. His eyes landed on Steve, and a flicker of curiosity crossed his face. He shot a quick glance at Raquel, who avoided her father's gaze for a second too long.

Camila caught on quickly. She stepped toward Steve, offering his hand. "And who is this fine young man?" she asked with a warm smile.

Raquel hesitated, her cheeks flushing. "Uh, this is Steve," she said, her voice slightly higher pitched than usual. "He's… my partner. We've been living together for a few years now."

Camila's face broke into a wide smile. "Steve! Well, it's wonderful to meet you," she said, stepping forward to give him a welcoming hug. "We were wondering when Raquel would finally bring someone home. She's so secretive!"

Steve relaxed visibly in Camila's warmth, then, shaking Julio's hand firmly, said: "It's a pleasure to meet you both. Raquel has told me so much about you."

"Not enough, apparently," Julio teased, giving Raquel a playful nudge. "Living together for three years and not a word? What are we, strangers?"

Raquel groaned, shooting a glare at David and Andrea, who were struggling to suppress their laughter. "I knew you'd make this a thing," she muttered.

Andrea grinned. "A thing? Raquel, they're not exactly traditionalists. You act like you've been hiding some scandal."

"Exactly!" David chimed in. "Mom and Dad are cooler than you give them credit for. I mean, come on, Dad listens to indie podcasts about urban farming."

Julio chuckled, throwing his arm around Camila. "He's not wrong. I learned a few tricks to work into the restaurant's menu with those podcasts."

Camila looked Steve over with an approving smile. "Well, Steve, any man who can put up with our Raquel is welcome in this family. Come inside, everyone. You must be hungry after the trip."

They all made their way into the house; Steve was visibly relieved by the warm reception. As they settled into the living room, drinks and snacks appeared, and the idle chatter resumed.

Andrea caught Raquel's eye and gave her a small smile. "See? Told you they wouldn't care."

Raquel rolled her eyes but smiled back. "Fine. You win. But don't think I'll let you off easy the next time you have a secret."

David laughed. "Oh, this family and secrets? We're practically professionals."

Julio, overhearing, raised an eyebrow. "Secrets, huh? Well, let's get them all out in the open before dinner, shall we? No surprises at the table."

The siblings exchanged a glance; Andrea subtly gripped the compass in her pocket. She knew the biggest secret of all wasn't about Raquel and Steve. It was about why they were here, what the compass was leading them toward, and the secrets they were about to reveal.

Chapter 18

Figuring It Out

The aroma of café con leche mingled with the wonderful smell of sizzling bacon, scrambled eggs, and freshly baked Cuban bread as Andrea and Steve stepped into the kitchen. Julio stood at the stove, expertly working on a pan of scrambled eggs with onions and sweet red peppers, while her mother was slicing the bread and chatting with Raquel.

Raquel, still in her pyjamas and turning towards Mark, was explaining the virtues of her favourite dish—ropa vieja¬—who looked half intrigued and half overwhelmed. He hoped, while the food sounded interesting, it did not seem appropriate for breakfast food.

"Mark," Andrea's father interjected with a teasing grin, "if you're going to marry into this family, you'd better learn how to make a proper flan. It's a rite of passage. You should help me make one for lunch to along the ropa vieja Raquel was describing."

"Marry?" Raquel choked on her coffee; eyes wide. "Whoa, let's not get ahead of ourselves, Papá!"

Everyone laughed, but Raquel knew he was just trying to gauge how serious things were between Raquel and Mark.

Meanwhile, David and Lisa walked into the room.

"Morning, everyone," David said as he sat down.

Lisa offered a much more chipper, "Good morning!" as she walked over to Julio to smell the scrambled eggs just as Camila said. "Sit, sit, all of you. Eat before it gets cold."

As everyone settled around the table, plates of food were passed back and forth, and everyone was piling food on their plates with a sense of gusto. As each finished their food, the conversation inevitably turned into a discussion as to why they were all here: the compass.

Raquel glanced at Andrea. "Did you figure out anything new about the compass since last night?"

Andrea shook her head. "Not really. It's like…it wants us to do something, but I have no clue what. I mean, it's a compass. It points, but to what?"

"Maybe it's broken," David said through a mouthful of food. Lisa swatted his arm.

"Broken or not," Steve chimed in, "it's the weirdest thing I've ever seen. Where did you even find it?"

Andrea hesitated, then said, "Our abuelo— our grandfather—gave it to us when we left Cuba. Abuelo said when we all turned 25, it would point us to a treasure, and now it is pointing south. I am guessing Cuba."

"Well, maybe we should find out once and for all," Raquel said, setting her fork down. Her voice carried a note of determination. "What if it's pointing us to go to Cuba?"

David groaned. "You're not seriously suggesting we go on some kind of wild treasure hunt, are you?"

"Why not?" Andrea shot back.

The room went quiet for a moment, save for the clinking of utensils. Then Andrea, with a mischievous smile, said, "I mean, we've got the time. Who's in?"

Before anyone could answer Camila, who had been quietly sipping her coffee, raised an eyebrow and asked, "Wait a minute. Are we just glossing over the fact that the compass might be pointing you to Communist Cuba? Tell me, or rather share with us, how exactly do you plan to get there? You can't just hop on a flight and start treasure hunting."

Julio looked at Andrea and said: "Andrea, your mother has an excellent point, you know. Getting into Cuba isn't exactly a walk in the park. Especially if you're travelling from the USA."

Raquel leaned back in her chair and chimed in: "It's not impossible, though. People visit Cuba all the time, don't they? Special tour, journalists, family members…"

"Sure, they must go to Cuba for very specific circumstances," Camila cut in. "Americans can only go for certain approved reasons such as education, or family visits, maybe some humanitarian work. Last I checked, 'chasing down a magical compass' isn't on the list."

Mark quipped: "Couldn't we frame it as a cultural research project or something? You know, document our findings about…what was it called? The glowing compass?"

"Sí, sí, I am sure Cuban customs will wave you right through with that explanation," added Julio.

"Thanks for that comment, Papá, not helping here. Okay, so what's the alternative?" Andrea asked, her brows furrowed. "We can't just ignore it. What if the compass is leading us to something important?"

Julio sighed and set his coffee down. "If you're serious about this, and I can't believe I'm even saying this, you'll need someone who knows the ropes. You'd need a guide, someone who knows the right channels, the right people."

The table fell silent as his words sunk in.

"I know someone who will help us," Julio said. "An old friend who is still in La Habana now working for the Cuban government."

Everyone stared at him. "Whoa, wait, what?" Andrea asked, her eyes wide. "You know someone in Cuba who will help. Who? How can a communist you know from way back then help us get into Cuba?"

Julio shrugged and just added: "He can, and he will."

Raquel looked sceptical. "You've been holding out on us, Papá."

"I am not holding out," Julio answered. "I never thought I would contact him again, but life has a way of coming back to you. And apparently, the time is now."

"But why would this communist friend of yours help us?" David asked, his tone still dubious. "We're just some random group of people chasing after a glowing compass."

Julio leaned forward, his voice lowering. "Because this friend owes me a favour. A big one."

The room buzzed with a mix of excitement and apprehension. Camila was the first to break the tension. "Okay, fine. Say we do this. How are we going to explain this to customs, our jobs, our families? And how do we even fund something like this?"

Andrea glanced at Raquel, then at David. "We'll figure it out. We always do, and I like the idea of a cultural research project like Mark mentioned."

Raquel raised her coffee cup. "To figuring it out."

The others hesitated, then followed suit. Even Camila couldn't help but smile as she clinked her mug against the others.

"To figuring it out," they all echoed.

Andrea felt a thrill of excitement surge through her. Whatever the compass had in store, they were in it together. And that, she thought, was the most important part.

Chapter 19

Steve's College Skill Set

After finishing dinner and cleaning up, the family gathered around the dining table just like Julio had asked. Julio had an expression on his face of both seriousness and curiosity. The siblings and their partners, on the other hand, were barely containing their giggles, having conspired earlier to present their most outlandish "secrets."

Julio cleared his throat. "Alright, everyone. I said I wanted all our family secrets on the table tonight, even you, Lisa, Mark, and Steve. No holding back. If we're going to undertake something as crazy as following this compass to Cuba, I need to know there are no surprises. Understood?"

Andrea smirked, exchanging a knowing glance with Raquel. "Understood, Papá," she said sweetly.

David was the first to go. He leaned forward: "Okay, I've been keeping this from you all for years, but…I'm actually the reason Mom's favourite vase broke when we were kids. I blamed it on the cat."

Julio rolled his eyes. "Por Dios, David, that's the best you've got?"

"Wait, wait, I'm not done," David said, holding up a hand. He could barely hold back his laughter as he tried to remember the story, he'd come up with an hour ago. "The twist is, there was no cat. I made it up. We never even had a cat."

Laughter erupted around the table, except for Julio, who rubbed his temples. "This is what I get for asking."

Next, Raquel chimed in, her tone equally dramatic. "Fine, my turn. I've been secretly practicing ventriloquism. I plan to quit my job as a lecturer at NYU and make it big in the puppet scene."

Even Steve, her ever-supportive partner, snorted at this. "She's lying, but honestly, I'd pay to see that."

Andrea, not to be outdone, raised her hand. "Okay, my turn. I've been running a secret underground pickle-tasting society. Our motto is, 'In brine we trust.'"

"Enough with the jokes. I said I wanted serious answers!"

Steve cleared his throat.

"Actually, sir, I do have a small secret. Back in my college days, I had this side hustle where I created fake personas for people. You know, like crafting elaborate backstories for passports, fake IDs, driver's licenses, things like that. I think this might, just might, solve our Cuba problem. What do you think, Mr Morales?"

"Steve, no more 'Mr Morales'; call me Julio from now on. OK?"

Nodding, Steve answered, "Yes, sir… Julio."

Raquel was totally surprised and shot him a look. "Steve, what are you talking about?"

"Let me finish," he said, holding up a finger. "I once helped this guy pose as a botanist researching rare tropical plants. I totally made up the credentials, the cover story, everything, just borrowed pieces from here and there from different real people, you know. The guy managed to get into Cuba for three weeks under the guise of collecting data on indigenous flora."

Staring at Steve Camila blurted out, "You're telling me you can create a fake backstory convincing enough to get us into Cuba?" Camila asked, totally flabbergasted by Steve's story.

Steve grinned. "I'm saying I can try. We'd need to pick something believable, though. Something that makes sense for a group like ours."

Camila said: "Like what?"

Steve thought for a moment and then said: "Well, the compass could be our angle. We claim we're researching its historical significance. Say it's tied to an old Cuban artifact or legend. We pose as a team of historians, archaeologists, and cultural experts."

David chuckled. "I call dibs on being the 'tech guy.' Every expedition needs one of those. I will make a website for us. I'll call it 'The Relic Raiders'. Catchy, right?"

"And what to do we do about funding?" Andrea asked.

"We could pitch it as a joint venture," Steve said. "Find a small grant for cultural research, but I think the best way, in my opinion, is to pool our resources. That way there'll be fewer people looking and maybe questioning our story. Worst case, we do some crowdfunding. People love throwing money at a good treasure hunt."

Julio, who had been listening intently, finally spoke. "As ridiculous as this all sounds…there's a chance it could work. If you're careful and don't draw too much attention."

Raquel nudged Steve playfully. "You've been holding out on me, Mr. Secret Agent."

Steve winked. "What can I say? I'm full of surprises. A man of many talents,"

Andrea sat back in her chair and had some concerns which she voiced right away. "Listen," she said, raising her voice just enough to cut through the chatter, "I love the idea, Steve. I really do. But if anyone's going to Cuba, it should be us. The siblings and our partners. Not Papá and Mamá. They're not exactly in their twenties anymore."

"What are you saying, Andrea? That your parents are too old for an adventure?" said Julio with Camila nodding her head a bit.

"No," Andrea said gently. "I'm saying it's too dangerous for you two. This isn't some guided tour; it's going back to Cuba—a Communist country, with a long memory. We can't risk it."

Raquel nodded in agreement. "Andrea's right. It's not just about age, Papá. You seem to have history there, Papá. People might recognise you. Your so-called friend that owes you a favour might not be as grateful to return the favour you did for him. That could complicate things."

Julio frowned but didn't argue, while their mother, Camila, raised a hand to calm everyone down. "Alright, let's stop yelling and think this through."

"Exactly," David interjected. "Besides, if anything goes wrong, it's easier for younger people to, uh, run."

"Dios mío," Camila said, rolling her eyes. "You're not making this better, David." She sighed. "Fine. We won't go. If this really is about the compass and your sibling bond, then it should be your journey, not ours."

Julio protested, but Camila gave him a look. The look only a husband knew how to react to. "Mi amor, let them do this. You've done enough crazy things for one lifetime."

"Alright," was his short answer.

"We will," Andrea promised. "We'll plan everything down to the last detail. We'll be careful."

Camila, now looking at her children with a mixture of worry and pride, added, "We'll help you get started. Julio and I will pitch in to partially fund this crazy idea, but you kids will need to handle the rest. Deal?"

Andrea glanced at her siblings. Raquel nodded decisively, David shrugged with a smirk, and Andrea finally said, "Deal."

Steve leaned back and with a big grin added: "Looks like we're officially in the treasure-hunting business."

By the end of the night, the table was strewn with notes, maps, and half-formed plans. Looking at the time on her watch, Raquel decided it was time for bed. More planning could be discussed in the morning, and they all agreed.

As Andrea and Mark stood to clear the plans and papers, Andrea glanced at her mother. "You sure you're okay with this, Mamá?"

Camila gave her a small smile and patted her hand. "No, but sometimes being a parent means letting your children take risks. Just promise me one thing."

"Anything."

"Be safe and come back; all of you, in one piece."

Andrea nodded: "We will, Mamá. I promise."

As she and Mark got ready for bed, she looked at him, ready to go to Cuba with her, for her. She was so lucky, and so were her siblings.

Andrea said to Mark: "You know, Steve's bizarre college skill set might just work."

Mark just answered: "Come to bed, sexy. Let me look for your treasure."

With a big grin, she took her clothes off and jumped in bed.

Chapter 20

Flying to Cuba

They could sense the hum of the airport terminal lights that cast a cool glow over the waiting area as the six of them sat together, speaking in hushed tones. Their Delta flight to La Habana was delayed by thirty minutes, giving them extra time to discuss their plans. The excitement was palpable, though it was tempered by an undercurrent of nervousness.

Andrea repeated what they had gone over the previous night.

She had laid the map of Cuba on the kitchen table and the compass needle point to La Habana and then to Baracoa as her finger traced the line toward Baracoa. "We know the compass points here, but we still don't know what it's leading us to."

"Treasure, obviously, I'm thinking gold coins, maybe a chest filled with emeralds," said David with a big smile.

Raquel interjected, "OK, let's slow down a bit and not get ahead of ourselves here. It could also just be something completely different. Like a relic or a historical artifact."

"You are right, Raquel," added Steve. "It could be as simple as a symbol or a relic. Nothing of value. Remember the research we read? Baracoa is rich in history with its indigenous legends, early Spanish settlements, and old customs. This could be about uncovering anything at all."

Mark smirked. "Well, if it is gold, I'm not complaining. It would be super cool! But I must admit I wonder sometimes if the compass might just be wrong. It could just be malfunctioning."

Andrea shook her head. "No way, Mark. Is the glow a malfunction as well? You saw how it glowed the morning of my 25th birthday, just like my abuelo said it would, well sort off. It was a sign. It is going to lead us somewhere; I just know it. It pointed to Baracoa the second we put it over the map. This isn't some cheap trinket."

Raquel chimed in. "OK, people. Let's settle down a bit. Let's not get ahead of ourselves. First, we need to get there safely and without raising any red flags. Remember what our dad said: Blend in."

Raquel now had her deep lectures' voice on and added: "The last thing we need is for someone to figure out we're not just here for 'professional research.'"

David added: "Do we all remember our cover stories? Because the Cuban authorities will ask."

Mark chuckled. "I'm the cultural researcher investigating historical trade routes, and Raquel is my expert on antiques and artifacts."

Raquel nodded. "Steve and I are focusing on the geographic and ecological impact of early exploration. And you, Andrea? Are you comfortable enough?"

"Hey sis. I am a professional photographer and documentarian," she said with a wink. "I've got the necessary cameras to prove it. Besides, I always bring a small portfolio to show off my immense talent."

That statement brought a few chuckles, but Steve frowned slightly. "We must be careful not to overplay our roles. If they sense we're just making this up, our heads are going to roll."

"Of course," David said. "Look, I got my cover all ready and set. I'm a tech specialist documenting the use of compasses in navigation. Super legit and Lisa is my assistant. Documenting everything."

"Very convincing," Andrea teased, her voice dripping with sarcasm.

"They won't," Raquel said firmly. "We've prepared for this. Plus, we've got all the paperwork, thanks to Steve and Papá's contact. It'll be fine."

The announcement for their flight crackled over the intercom, and they all exchanged glances. It was finally time.

As they stood and gathered their belongings, Mark asked, "Alright, so let's say we get to La Habana with no issues. What's the first step?"

Andrea reiterated what she said when she'd placed the compass over the map of Cuba on the kitchen table. "We let the compass lead us on the way to Baracoa."

"You know, little sister, this is not exactly a foolproof plan," David muttered, though his grin betrayed his excitement.

"No," Andrea said, smiled. "But it's the best plan we've got."

As they boarded the plane, their conversations shifted to lighter topics. Places they wanted to explore, food they couldn't wait to try. Maybe even go to their old house in La Habana without raising suspicions and visit the cemetery where their grandparents were buried. All if they had the time and were not followed t Pal by the authorities. Their father's "friend" promised no close supervision by the authorities. How he managed that, they never questioned, but they would remain alert for suspicious individuals during their visit.

But the weight of their mission lingered in the back of their minds. Baracoa awaited, and with it, whatever secrets the compass was guiding them toward.

Chapter 21
Mojitos

Arriving at the airport, they were immediately hit with the heat and humidity. A mix of relief and exhilaration settled over the group after clearing customs without a hitch. They spotted a man near the baggage claim area holding a sign that read "Morales Party."

The man holding the sign was tall, dark, and handsome in his mid-twenties. He carried himself with a neatly trimmed beard and a warm smile. As they approached, he greeted them in Spanish. "Bienvenidos a La Habana. Mi nombre es Manuel Borrageors. El señor Tomas me ha pedido que los recoja. ¿Son ustedes la familia de Julio Morales?"

"Yes, that's us," Andrea whispered, nudging Raquel.

The siblings introduced themselves and their partners, and after a quick exchange of pleasantries, Manuel now spoke with his broken English, saying he wished to practice his English and asked if it was OK with them as he gestured toward the exit. "Come. Your cars are waiting. Sorry, no minibus," he said with a chuckle. "But we'll travel in style."

Outside, three gleaming 1950s sedans were parked at the curb, their vibrant pastel colours shining in the tropical sun. One was a Cadillac, another a Chevrolet, and finally a Ford. The group paused, taken aback by the classic cars.

"Are you serious?" David said, grinning as he took in the spectacle. "This is amazing."

Manuel smirked. "This is Cuba. We may not have the newest cars, but we make them last."

The group divided into the three cars, forming a conga line as Manuel took the lead in the Chevy. The convoy wove through the streets of Havana, now totally unrecognisable to the siblings since they had left so long ago. The old-world charm of the city was still undeniable, with its colonial architecture, but many building showed signs of decay and needed repairs.

Their destination was the Kempinski Manzana, a luxurious five-star hotel in the city's heart. The group collectively gasped as they pulled up to the grand building, its modern elegance blending seamlessly with Havana's historical charm. What a difference between the life of 'normal Cubans' and the 'turistas'.

Manuel and the other drivers helped them with their luggage as they checked in. "Please, please. Go to your rooms, unpack, relax and meet me at the bar afterward. We'll discuss the itinerary," Manuel suggested.

The group agreed, each heading to their respective rooms. The accommodations were impeccable, with polished marble floors, plush bedding, and balconies offering views of the bustling city.

An hour later, they gathered in the hotel's rooftop bar, which offered views of old La Habana as the sun was getting ready to set, and they settled into a large table and ordered mojitos.

Andrea raised her mojito, her voice light but filled with purpose. "To making it this far. And to an excellent research paper."

The others lifted their glasses in agreement. "To the research," Raquel added with a grin.

They had agreed on the plane, not to mention the compass to anyone and, not being sure if there was any eavesdropping in the hotel, they would, as much as possible, speak in code.

Manuel appeared as if on cue. He pulled up a chair and placed a map of Cuba on the table on the table. "I've made arrangements for our trip east in a minibus," he began, his tone serious. "The journey to Baracoa will take time and money, which I need as soon as possible. And I will let you know the trip itself will not be without its challenges. Are you able to pay now in Cuban pesos to take you there and the same amount to pick you up and return to La Habana? It will be a total of 7,000 Cuban pesos."

"What?" exclaimed David. "That is nothing but highway robbery?"

The group started almost shouting until Lisa put a stop to it.

"Wait a second, guys," she said, reaching for her purse.

"Here," and she counted out the 3,500 pesos and handed them to Manual who smiled each time a bill landed on his hand.

"Señorita," said Manuel, "you stopped too soon. I need 7,000 pesos."

"No, Manuel. Half now and half when we return. That is, it. Take it or leave it," Lisa said in the politest manner.

Nodding and smiling, Manuel said: "Sí, sí, Señorita. We leave at 8AM the day after tomorrow. Now, let me show you the route and the stops. The trip will take about eighteen hours because of the roads, but I will drive safe for you."

The group leaned in and looked at the map and the stops. Eighteen hours were on their mind, but their excitement was mingling with a touch of apprehension. They were finally here, on the cusp of the finding the answer to the compass.

After Manuel finished, he said his goodbyes and the group ordered another round of mojitos and the conversation exploded.

"Lisa, you spent 3,500 Cuban pesos on what, exactly? Are we secretly funding a revolution I didn't know about?" demanded Raquel.

"Please tell me it wasn't for something ridiculous like another scarf that changes colours in the sun," remarked David.

Rolling her eyes, Lisa took a sip of her mojito. "It wasn't a scarf. And calm down, it's not as bad as it sounds. It's only like 150 USD."

Andrea reacted in astonishment. "Wait, 3,500 pesos equals $150? That math isn't working for me. How does that even work?"

"It's just the exchange rate, Andrea. Cuban pesos are super devalued compared to the US dollar right now," answered Lisa, "and as keeper of the funds as voted before we left, I did plenty of research, so I saw a bargain and I took it."

"Okay, but what was it for? Are we talking about necessity or luxury? Because $3,500 of anything better be gilded in gold."

"It was a necessity and a bargain. Plane rides are almost impossible to obtain on short notice and besides, as you saw from Manuel's map, he has made arrangements, such as rest stops, and food included on the way to and back from Baracoa. So, since we are not locals, I thought it was a good value for our money."

Mark interjected. "Lisa, are we getting scammed here by Manuel? He did smile a lot when you were placing the bills in his greedy little hands."

Lisa took the last sip of her mojito before she answered him. "Mark, no, I do not believe we were being scammed. I am sure Manuel is getting a cut from the 3,500 pesos, and remember, he wanted the entire 7,000 pesos upfront, and I said no to that idea. I think everyone involved will have a share. It is how it works here and in every country in the world. Everyone gets a cut."

"Now that you explained how it works 3,500 or rather 7,000, it doesn't sound like highway robbery," added Steve, also taking the last of his drink.

"You know, it still felt like highway robbery. This highway just happens to be in Cuba, but," David added with a grin, "my

Lisa is quite a negotiator and funds manager, am I right?" He raised his almost empty glass of mojito.

Lisa grinned and added: "Well, we will be in a Cuban minibus for eighteen hours together. How bad can that be?"

"How bad can that be?" repeated Andrea, "Eighteen hours. I hope it comes with a minibar, this minibus!"

They all laughed at Andrea's remark and Mark added: "Come, folks, I am sure we'll complain about everything during this trip. Let's order one final round of drinks and some food because it will probably be a while before we are sipping on the best mojitos in town."

Chapter 22

Sightseeing

Morning came, and the group met for breakfast, and even after having a delicious and late dinner, they were all starving. Steve made a comment, which everyone agreed with. Slapping his stomach he said: "I am looking like a small version of buddha."

"OK, do not get me started Steve," said Lisa as she whipped out her purse.

"Here's 2,000 pesos each. Don't lose it, don't spend it all in one place, and I expect every single peso you don't use back when we meet tonight for dinner and a rehash of our one-day adventure in La Habana."

Giving Lisa a mock salute, David said: "Yes, Supreme Overlord Lisa. Shall I bow now, or when I hand over the leftover coins?"

With a slight snicker Raquel added in: "Yeah, Lisa, lighten up. It's not like we're going to blow it all on cigars and rum. Well, maybe David might."

"David will be with me all day and I'm serious! This isn't Monopoly money, people. Let's not embarrass ourselves."

With a big grin on her face, Andrea interjected: "Don't worry, Your Highness. We'll even keep receipts if it pleases the Crown."

"I don't think many places will give receipts here. I guess you will have trust us," said Steve.

Steve did an impersonation of a British butler and added: "Madam, if we're late, shall we flog ourselves, or will you handle the punishments personally?"

Lisa just rolled her eyes. "Just be back here by 7 tonight so we can have dinner. No excuses. And no getting arrested."

As they exited the hotel, each of the couples jumped into a one of the marvellous ancient American cars and left.

David and Lisa told their driver to take them to El Malecón, Habana's famous seaside promenade, where they were dropped off.

There they walk the long promenade and stop to see some street performers, musicians, and even a guy pretending to be a human statue.

"Do you think he'd break character if I poked him?" David asked Lisa, laughing.

"Please don't, David. I don't want to end up in a viral video titled "Annoying Tourists in Habana"."

They stopped at a small café overlooking the ocean for lunch. David, ever the adventurer, ordered a dish he couldn't remember how to pronounce, while Lisa opted for a safe choice of ropa, having enjoyed it at Camila's place in Miami. Afterwards, as they walked, David tried bargaining with a vendor for a hat that was clearly too small for him.

"You look ridiculous haggling. Just pay the guy what he's asking."

"Where's the fun in that? Bargaining is part of every country's cultural experience!"

They ended their day at the Castillo de los Tres Reyes del Morro, taking photos and arguing over who had the better phone camera.

Meanwhile, Raquel and Steve veered toward the more artistic side of Old Havana. Their first stop was the Fábrica de Arte Cubano, an eclectic space filled with galleries, live music, and experimental art and afterward they strolled through the Plaza Vieja, stopping to buy handcrafted jewellery and locally made leather goods. Steve couldn't resist posing for pictures in front of the colourful colonial buildings, striking exaggerated "artistic" poses that made Raquel laugh so hard she almost dropped her camera.

They ended their day at a small rooftop bar, sipping mojitos and watching the sun set over the city before rushing back for dinner.

Steve raised his mojito and toasted: "To not getting lost and spending less than Lisa thought we would."

Clicking their glasses Raquel added: "And to proving her wrong when she asks for change tonight."

Andrea and Mark explored the Mercado de San José, a massive artisan market filled with paintings, wood carvings, and textiles. Andrea haggled for a vibrant, hand-painted canvas while Mark got distracted by a booth selling vintage postcards.

"Would you look at this, Andrea? It is an old photo of 1950s Habana! I feel like I just stepped into a time machine."

Remembering a little bit of her youth in Cuba, Andrea just smiled and looked at the old photo.

Next, they wandered into La Habana Vieja, exploring narrow cobblestone streets and chatting with locals. They stumbled upon a hidden café where a band was playing traditional Cuban music. Mark convinced Andrea to dance, even though neither of them knew the steps.

"Mark, you're terrible at this."

Mark grinned . "And yet you're still dancing."

Their last stop was El Capitolio, the grand government building that looked like it had been plucked straight out of Washington, D.C. Mark tried, and failed, to convince Andrea to climb up for a better view.

With a big laugh Andrea just said, "The only thing you're climbing is Lisa's list of enemies if we're late. Let's grab some coffee and head back we do not want to be late."

Later that evening, they all met for dinner, and everyone shared their adventures of the day.

After ordered and before the meals arrived, Lisa went into control mode: "All right, cough it up. How much did you all waste?"

Raquel quickly answered: "Waste? We call it investing in memories, thank you. And let's just say the real treasure was the experiences we had along the way," she said as she handed back 500 pesos.

"And by experiences, she means dancing terribly in front of strangers," quipped Mark and received a quick slap on the arm from Raquel.

As the laughter rang out, Lisa couldn't help but smile. Tyrant or not, it had been a day to remember.

Chapter 23

Road To Baracoa

Right on schedule the next morning, Manuel showed up with a minibus, a little worn, but it looked like it had good tyres. The three couples helped Manuel to load up their bags and Andrea's camera equipment. The minibus seated 30, so they had plenty of room to spread out. Manuel had the radio on, but the noise of the road hid some of the music and news. When asked to raise the volume, Manuel answered: "Sorry, it is at this level or off."

Manuel drove the minibus steadily along and they reach the outskirts of La Habana and the countryside open in front of them.

Heading east along the Carretera Central, which was Cuba's main highway, the group found that the first major stretch took them through Matanzas province, known for its beautiful Varadero beaches, though they were north of the primary route and so they could not stop to see.

They continued east; the views were beautiful and while Andrea wanted to take some photos Manuel said they could not because they needed to make time while on the road but added: "Alright, amigos. We'll be stopping soon for a quick breakfast. I know a place that serves the best café con leche this side of Cuba."

The group murmured in agreement, eager to stretch their legs and sample the local flavours. Raquel glanced back at her siblings, a smile tugging at her lips. It had been years since they'd taken a trip together, let alone with their partners.

They stopped right off the highway in a little store that did not even have a name, or at least they could not see a name on it, but at least they could stretch their legs and grab some café con leche and use the facilities. This took thirty minutes, and they hopped back into the minibus.

After a while, no one really seemed to watch the time. They went past Santa Clara, a city steeped in revolutionary history, home to the Che Guevara Mausoleum. Then the landscape really changed as they entered Cuba's agricultural heartland, with vast sugarcane fields and tobacco plantations dotting the countryside.

As they reached Camagüey, Cuba's third-largest city, Manuel said it was time for a light lunch. Camagüey had distinctive colonial architecture and an unusual street layout. It was purposefully designed as a maze to confuse pirates in colonial times, or so insisted Manuel. The city was famous for its many churches and its well-preserved historic center.

After they finished lunch, the trip continued through Las Tunas and into Holguín province, where the terrain became more dramatic as you approached the Sierra Maestra mountains. This mountain range, Cuba's highest, served as a hideout for Castro's revolutionary forces in the 1950s.

Stopping for dinner before the sunlight faded away, Manuel chose a café in Santiago de Cuba. Here he explained that they would then head over one of Cuba's most remarkable roads, La Farola. The road, explained Manuel, was a winding mountain highway, built in 1964, that cut through the mountains with dramatic switchbacks and offering breathtaking views of the coastline, but he added: "I am sorry you will not see much unless the moon is out tonight," which it was but the night sky was cloudy obscuring what would have been a delightful sight.

During this stretch of the road, the group was mostly to themselves. Raquel leaned against Steve, her head resting lightly on his shoulder. They silently hoped they could hear waves, but alas, the minibus was too noisy. David and Lisa, seated two rows directly behind them, were using a torch to pore over a travel guide, pointing out highlights of Baracoa they hoped to visit. Andrea and Mark, almost at the rear of the minibus, alternated between chatting and dozing off, lulled by the rhythmic motion of the bus.

Suddenly Manuel announced: "We are almost there. I am glad for I will sleep well tonight. Once we get there, I will help you unload, open the house and come back later today."

"So, our accommodations are ready for tonight? It is quite late. It is almost midnight," chimed in Raquel, having to almost yell from the rear of the minibus.

"Yes, señorita. I fixed everything. Do not worry. Manuel has taken care of everything. This house is where you will meet el Señor Geronimo Betancourt. He will meet you in the morning at 9AM."

"Manuel, do you know who he is?" Andrea asked.

"I was told he is the grandson of a man—Don Francisco—your grandfather knew. You do not recognise the name?"

"No," answered Raquel looking at her siblings who just shook their heads.

"Very well, do not worry. He is very punctual and knows a lot of history of Baracoa. I think he will be of help, yes?"

Once they arrived, the group unloaded the minibus, and they stumbled groggily into the small home Manuel had arranged for them. The house was cozy, its modest décor and welcoming air a testament to the thoughtfulness of their new friend.

"Señorita, here is the key—sorry only one key. There is food in the refrigerator and plenty of beans and rice and bread and coffee, oh, plenty of coffee for you. I see you later. Good night, or should I say buenos día." He closed the door behind him.

After some playful arguments about who would claim which bedroom, the six of them collapsed into their respective spaces, exhaustion overtaking excitement for the moment.

Raquel lay awake a little longer, sensing her siblings not falling asleep as well. Whatever lay ahead in Baracoa, she knew it was just the beginning of their journey.

Chapter 24

Gran Cemí of Patana

Raquel poured coffee into her mug; her eyes were barely open.

"So, let's recap. We've got ourselves a glowing compass that brought us to Cuba. We think said compass will lead us to a legendary treasure, and now we wait for a Geronimo Betancourt to come," She looked at her watch, "in exactly fifteen minutes to help us. Am I missing anything?"

Andrea, munching on a slice of toast, raised an eyebrow. "Don't forget that Señor Betancourt will probably come and look like a historian out of the pages of Indiana Jones."

David, flipping through a local newspaper and pretending to read, snorted. "It would have been better if Abuelo had told us that the compass is actually an alien artifact that glows when it is close to one—you know, something out of the X-Files like when we watched the show as kids."

"Excuse me for considering all possibilities," Andrea said, waving her butter knife like a sword. "Maybe the treasure is an alien artifact. Wouldn't that explain why Abuelo kept it secret?"

"Or maybe," Mark chimed in, "it's just old gold coins and he didn't want anyone looting his retirement fund. Honestly, Andrea, aliens?"

As they all laughed, a firm knock sounded at the door.

Steve opened the door and led Señor Betancourt into the room, his presence commanding yet warm. He looked exactly as they imagined. Crisp linen shirt, Panama hat, and a leather satchel slung over his shoulder. "Good morning, amigos! Are we ready to uncover history?"

Raquel whispered to Andrea, "Called it. He does have a hat."

Betancourt set his satchel on the table and began pulling out aged maps, a journal, and a compass that looked suspiciously like theirs. "Now, about this treasure. Your grandfather, Don Francisco, was not only a seeker of knowledge but also a man of great secrets. Rumour has it he found the legendary treasure of Gran Cemí of Patana."

Andrea raised her hand like a student. "Señor Betancourt, question: does this Gran Cemí of Patana treasure involve aliens?"

Betancourt paused, visibly thrown off. "Aliens? No, señorita. Why would you think that?"

David chuckled. "Don't ask. Please, just don't."

Betancourt continued. "The treasure is said to be more than gold. It is an artifact of unimaginable value, tied to the legacy of our ancestors."

"Everybody just stop for a second," spoke Steve.

Like a magnet, all heads, and eyes were on Steve, even Betancourt's.

"Now, I am not an archaeologist, but I read a lot, and I mean a lot, and I swear I read that this Gran Cemí of Patana or—as it is called in the States, the Idol of Patana—is one of the 157 million artifacts and specimen is currently at the Smithsonian in Washington D.C. so it could not be still in Cuba. It was taken to the USA in 1915 to 1917, I am now sure exactly, by someone named Mark something or other. I am fairly sure of that."

Raquel leaned in, intrigued. "So, what is this Gran Cemí of Patana or the Idol of Patana, whatever the name? What is it? A crown? A sceptre? A golden llama?"

Betancourt again took over the conversation: "It is said that the Idol of Patana is a stalagmite stone containing the face of a god. I never been to the USA, so I do not know, but the local rumours are that the stone has mystical powers. The idol legends say that at a certain hour of the morning, at least during June and July, a ray of sunlight illuminated the stone, highlighting the face that has been carved into the stone."

"Maybe it lights up for something else? Maybe it has been near something, a power source, a compass…." said David, which immediately aroused faces from Raquel and Andrea, which made David shy back a bit.

"I do not know," Betancourt stated, "My abuelo never figured out what your grandfather found, but I want to let you know that there is a complication. I was told that a man called Ramiro, he is a… how do you say… unpleasant individual?"

"Unpleasant?" David smirked. "That's a polite way of saying 'guy who stalks people and probably smells like cheese.'"

"Yes," Betancourt nodded gravely, missing the sarcasm. "He has been asking questions. He knows you are here and suspects you have the key to finding the treasure."

"Great," Andrea sighed. "We've officially become characters in a telenovela. What's next? A dramatic betrayal?"

Betancourt straightened, clearly not following her humour. "No, señorita. Next, we follow the clues your grandfather left behind. My grandfather, who knew your abuelo, documented everything except the actual location and the treasure. But I warn you, this will not be easy. The path is treacherous, the treasure well-hidden."

Raquel clapped her hands. "Perfect. We're up against the terrain, history, and a man named Ramiro who may or may not smell like cheese. Let's do this."

Betancourt smiled, tipping his hat. "I admire your enthusiasm. Shall we begin?"

The siblings exchanged glances. With a mix of excitement and dread, they all nodded.

Before they started studying the information Betancourt brought, Andrea added, "But seriously, if Ramiro starts speaking Klingon, I'm out."

Chapter 25

Connections

Raquel leaned forward after hearing the information from Betancourt. "So, you're saying most of this is based on your grandfather's research? Rumors and notes, nothing verified?"

Betancourt nodded. "That's right. My grandfather was the real historian in the family. I'm just the caretaker of his work, and ophthalmologist by education, but let me show you what I found as I looked through the old papers." He pulled a paper from his satchel and placed it on the table. "I stumbled upon something unexpected."

Raquel's brow furrowed in suspicion. "What kind of 'something'?"

Pulling out a faded envelope sealed with brittle, yellowed wax, he said: "This. It was tucked inside an old journal. I hadn't noticed it before, and the seal was still intact. Like it had never been opened. So, naturally, I opened it."

"What did it say? What did your grandfather write?" asked David.

"I didn't know it would be relevant to you until I read it," Betancourt answered as he unfolded a single sheet of paper from the envelope and smoothed it on the table. The siblings leaned closer to read over his shoulder.

Scrawled in elegant but faint handwriting were the words:

"To uncover the truth, follow the light of the rising sun. Seek the edge where land greets the sea, where the East calls and secrets awaken."

"The rising sun? The East? Are you saying this is pointing us to the easternmost part of Cuba?" quipped Steve.

"That's what it seems to suggest," Betancourt said. "I cross-referenced the note with some of my grandfather's maps. If we're interpreting this correctly, it's referring to Punta de Maisí. The very tip of the island."

Andrea's face lit up with excitement. "The lighthouse! Isn't there a famous one there? What if it's connected?"

David frowned. "We're jumping to conclusions. This could just be poetic nonsense."

"Could be," she picked up the paper, scrutinizing it. "But considering everything we've seen so far, it's worth a look."

"The compass," Andrea chimed in, "maybe it'll react there! It has done little since we arrived, but what if this is what it's been waiting for?"

Betancourt leaned back in his chair, observing their animated discussion with a small smile. "Compass? What compass?"

Andrea looked at her siblings, who nodded their approval, and took out the compass from her purse.

Betancourt looked at it. "This looks exactly like the compass I inherited from my grandfather. What is so special about it?"

"Señor Betancourt, has your compass ever glowed?"

Betancourt looked at Andrea and made a face. "Glow? Of course, it does not even work. It points nowhere like a compass should I kept it all these years as a sentimental reminder of my abuelo. Does yours glow señorita, Andrea?"

Andrea went and told Betancourt the story of how they received their compass from their grandfather and what has transpired over the years, and how the compass was the reason as to why they were now in Cuba.

Betancourt smiled and just said: "Well, it sounds like you three are ready for an adventure."

"We are," answered Raquel, "but if we're going all the way to Punta de Maisí, from what you said, we'll need to prepare. It's not exactly a short trip from here."

"Leave that to me," Betancourt said. "I can arrange transport and supplies. But you should know this the area is remote. Few tourists go out there, and it has its challenges. The Indigenous people living there, the descendants of the Taínos, still believe in the old legends. Stories about buried treasures, ghosts, and... other things."

"Other things?" Andrea raised an eyebrow.

Betancourt shrugged, clearly enjoying the suspense. "You'll see. Let's just say it's a place where the past and the present meet and feel connected somehow."

Raquel exchanged glances with her siblings. David sighed, muttering under his breath about how this felt like chasing shadows, but even he couldn't entirely hide his curiosity.

"Alright," Raquel said. "We'll go. We hope this does not lead us on a wild goose chase. If it does, Señor Betancourt, you're buying us dinner."

Betancourt chuckled. "Deal. But your grandfather's compass, this note. It's all connected. I can feel it."

Betancourt, the siblings, and their partners moved to the lounge and got themselves some drinks, mostly Cuban rum over ice, and continued discussing their plans for the journey.

No one noticed the faint glow of Francisco's compass as it lay on top of the map on the table, as if it were anticipating what lay ahead.

Chapter 26

Ramiro

The Sierra Maestra stretched endlessly before them, its rugged peaks crowned by mist and dense foliage. The path was treacherous, uneven rocks, tangled roots, and steep inclines that tested them all. Raquel's breath came in heavy bursts as she adjusted her pack for the third time that hour.

"Betancourt, you still think this is a great idea?" Raquel muttered, glaring at him. The man looked perfectly at ease, not a concern, as if he was not even affected by the trek.

Andrea, walking alongside Pedro, a wiry man with a quick smile and a knack for spotting the safest paths that Betancourt brought along, chuckled at Raquel's annoyance. "I think he's secretly part mountain goat," Pedro commented with a smile.

Pablo, Pedro's cousin just smiled and added: "No, he's just too stubborn to get tired. Sierra Maestra can chew up and spit out anyone, but not him."

Pedro whispered but everyone seemed to have heard him. "It's the mountains. They humble everyone eventually."

They trudged on the challenging terrain, and they looked at the diverse jungle that was the Sierra Maestra until they reach a spot and Betancourt simple announced: "We'll camp here for the night."

After setting up camp and started a few small fires crackled, the group shared stories over simple meals of rice, beans, and dried meat. Pedro entertained them with tales of local legends: spirits of guerrilleros, Castro's men who died for the revolution, still haunted the mountains, and treasure hunters who vanished without a trace. Lisa could not help herself and shared Halloween stories which the three Cuban men found amusing but interesting at the same time.

After Lisa's stories David, ever the sceptic, rolled his eyes. "Spirits and treasure hunters? Sounds like you're trying to scare us from going forward."

"Believe what you want, mi amigo," Pedro said, shrugging. "But these mountains remember everything, and they never forgive."

Andrea shivered, moving closer to the fire, closer to Mark. Raquel, however, was more focused on the compass in Andrea's hand. Its faint glow had grown stronger with each step eastward. "Was she the only one that noticed it that?" she thought to herself.

On the fourth day, just as the group descended into a dense valley, Betancourt exchanged with Pedro and Pablo. Moments later, they all heard it: voices. Low, gruff, and too close for comfort.

"Get down!" Betancourt yelled, pulling Raquel down, followed by Steve. The others followed suit, crouching low as three armed men emerged from the trees.

The leader, a burly man with a scar slicing through his left eyebrow, raised his rifle. "You're a long way from any tourist trail," he growled. "Looking for something, maybe?"

"Ramiro," Betancourt muttered under his breath.

"You know him?" Raquel whispered.

"Unfortunately."

Ramiro stepped closer, his gaze narrowing on the group. "Hand over the compass. Now."

Raquel's heart pounded. "How does he know about the compass?" she whispered.

"Long story," Betancourt said, his voice tight. "Not one we have time for."

Pedro and Pablo exchanged glances. Without a word, Pablo subtly shifted his machete behind his back. Andrea caught the movement and whispered, "What's the plan?"

Pablo smiled faintly. "Survive."

Ramiro barked out a command, and his associates moved closer. At that moment, Pablo lunged. His machete struck the rifle of one man, knocking it away. Chaos erupted as Pedro tackled the other, and the group scattered.

"Run!" Betancourt shouted, grabbing Raquel's arm.

Gunshots rang out, but the dense forest offered cover. The group sprinted, branches clawing at their clothes and faces. Andrea clutched the compass tightly, her breath ragged as Mark followed her.

"Split up!" Betancourt yelled, guiding Raquel, Steve, Andrea, and Mark down a steep slope. Pedro and Pablo led the others in another direction, creating confusion.

By the time the gunfire ceased, the group regrouped at a hidden clearing, panting and shaken. The compass, still in Andrea's grasp, continued its glow as steady as ever.

Betancourt wiped his brow, his usual calm demeanour slipping. "Ese bastardo estuvo terriblemente cerca," looking at both Pedro and Pablo, who nodded in agreement.

Raquel glared at him. "Who is this guy? Who is Ramiro, and how does he know about the compass?"

Betancourt hesitated. "He... let's just say he's been after my grandfather's research for years. I didn't think he'd follow us here."

Andrea crossed her arms. "You did not think that? You thought he was just a city criminal? That scar on his face tells me a lot about the man, and I do not want to meet up with him again."

"I didn't want to alarm you," Betancourt said. "But now we know he's here watching us and following. We have to move quickly."

Andrea held up the compass, its light still pulsing. "Then let's not waste any more time. Whatever's waiting for us, it will not wait forever."

Silence fell as they all stared at the glowing artifact, its mysterious pull drawing them deeper into the Sierra Maestra, and closer to the secrets it guarded.

Chapter 27

Coincidence

As the group pressed onward through the dense jungle, the siblings found themselves reminiscing about the past.

Andrea wiped the sweat from her brow and grinned at Raquel, and started a conversation, just to take away the challenges of the trek from their minds. "Remember that summer we camped in Abuela's backyard? We thought we were such explorers."

Raquel laughed, dodging a low-hanging branch. "How could I forget? We spent hours mapping out the garden, convinced there was buried treasure under the old tree."

"And David," Andrea continued, "insisted he was the leader of the expedition. He even made us call him Captain Morales."

David chuckled, though he winced as he adjusted his pack. "Captain Morales led you to the best stash of Abuela's empanadas, didn't he?"

"That is an excellent point, and I remember they were also very good empanadas," Andrea admitted with a big grin on her face.

Even Betancourt could not help but chime in with his own stories of his childhood. Pedro and Steveo listened with amusement, but they shared nothing with the group, which made Andrea hesitate a bit, but she forced herself not to worry about it.

As the sun dipped below the horizon, Betancourt gestured ahead. "Tomorrow morning, we'll reach the cave. The Cave of the Idol of Panata. If the compass is to be believed, that's where your journey ends."

Raquel frowned. "And if the legends are true. Whatever's waiting for us there won't be simple."

After helping to set up camp, Pedro and Pablo silently disappeared into the jungle.

"Where are those two going?" asked Mark.

"Not sure," answered Lisa. "Let's not worry about them and let us help prepare dinner instead. I am sure they will return soon."

Dinner was served and the two cousins had not returned, but two plates had been put to the side. After almost three hours, they returned, their faces were unreadable.

"We will sleep well tonight," Pedro said simply. "We've placed several precautions around the camp."

Before anyone could ask what, they meant, they sat down to eat, speaking little but keeping their weapons within reach.

The night was still and heavy with the scent of damp earth. The group had barely drifted into uneasy sleep when a blood-curdling scream tore through the silence. Everyone bolted upright, fumbling for their torches.

"What was that?" Andrea gasped, her voice trembling.

Pedro motioned for silence, his machete gleaming in the faint moonlight. "Stay close. Follow me."

They moved cautiously toward the sound, their torches casting eerie shadows in the thick foliage. The air grew colder as they approached a small clearing. There, illuminated by the stark beam of Raquel's torch, was Ramiro.

The once-formidable man was impaled on a makeshift lance, his lifeless eyes staring into nothingness. Blood pooled beneath him, dark and viscous, while the lance pierced his chest cleanly through the heart. His companions were nowhere to be seen.

Raquel turned away, her stomach churning. Andrea clung to David, her face pale. "What... who... did this?"

"His men ran," Pedro said grimly, scanning the area. "Cowards."

"Or smart," Steveo added quietly. "Something, or someone, got to them first."

Betancourt's expression said it all: "We can't leave him like this. Pedro. Pablo, you know what to do."

Raquel shook her head vehemently. "I'm not staying here another second. I am to go back to camp."

David, however, stayed rooted. "I'll help." He glanced at Betancourt. "Let's get it over with."

Pedro and Steveo worked quickly, their faces blank masks of efficiency. David and the two cousins dug a shallow grave near the clearing's edge.

When they returned to camp, David's face was solemn. He dropped his pack and simply said, "It's done. If the compass has a curse, it just claimed its victim."

Andrea shuddered. "David, please don't say that. It was horrible what we saw. It is probably just a coincidence."

Pedro and Steveo slowly exchanged glances but said nothing.

Their thoughts were in sync.

They both thought the same thing: Well, we had something to do with that.

The camp fell into silence, each member grappling with the horror of what they'd seen. Andrea clutched the glowing compass, its light faint but unwavering, as though urging them forward despite the mounting dread.

Tomorrow, they would reach the cave.

Chapter 28

Fake

The next morning, it took just a few hours to reach the cave. Betancourt motioned to the siblings to step in first. Lighting up their torches, the trio moved slowly, each inspecting the sides of the caves for any clues, followed by their partners and finally Betancourt and Pedro and Pablo.

"Nothing. There is nothing here," exclaimed David. "It all has been a waste of time and money," dejected he stated.

"There must be something. Abuelo gave us the compass. It glowed. It brought us here. It cannot be for nothing. Keep looking," Andrea almost pleaded.

Suddenly Lisa blurted out: "Look here. A slight break into the stone. Not too large, but large enough for a body to squeeze in. Shall we go in?"

The group gather outside of the opening and agreed that they had nothing to lose, but they needed to leave everything behind save for their torches. Pablo was tasked with staying behind with the equipment and then, in order of age, the siblings squeezed their way in, followed by their partners, Betancourt, and bringing up the rear, Pedro.

First in was Raquel, who led them and after a few minutes of scrapping herself by the old stones in the wall, she emerged into a hidden chamber, and what a chamber it was.

"It a chamber of sorts and it is enormous," was all Raquel could manage at the stunning sight.

The ceiling arched high above, adorned with intricate frescoes that told of ancient stories. Incredibly, the colours were still vibrant. Ten massive pillars, carved from stone, rise on their surfaces etched with age-old runes and symbols.

As the group stepped forward, their eyes went to the centre of the chamber, and they all stopped in awe at what they saw: a stone statue.

"It is the Gran Cemi de Patana," exclaimed Betancourt.

The Gran Cemi de Patana rested on an intricately carved pedestal. Its surface shimmered, resonating with the compass in Andrea's hand.

"This can't be real," Andrea whispered. "The Gran Cemi is in the Smithsonian. Right?"

"That is what Steve read and shared with us, right, Steve?"

"That is correct. I did read it, but I never seen it, so I do not know what to believe now," Steve mumbled.

"What if the Gran Cemi never left Cuba?" David proposed.

"What are you saying, David? You are not implying…." Raquel's voice trails off.

"I am saying that the one in Washington is a fake," David said, stepping closer to the artifact. "Think about it. This one looks untouched, pristine. It's hidden here, deep in this cave, in this enormous chamber, as if it has been protected over the centuries. Watched over by someone who has kept it immaculate all this time. Someone takes care of it."

Andrea shook her head, pacing. "But why would anyone go to such lengths to replace it with a fake? And who could've done it?"

Before David could answer, Pedro pointed to a small wooden chest tucked in the chamber's corner. It looked old but seemed sturdy enough, despite its age.

The compass in Andrea's hand dimmed slightly, as though no longer leading them. The Gran Cemi had been its destination, but the chest now demanded their attention.

Pedro knelt beside the chest, running his fingers over the Taino symbols etched into the wood. "This writing... it's Taíno," he murmured.

"Pedro, what does it say? Can you read it?" Andrea asked, leaning closer.

Pedro looked up and read the inscription. "Yes. It reads: Only the worthy may open. Inside lies the truth. Be ready."

Steve lets out a small chuckle: "Well, that's vague and ominous."

"Truths? What truths is it referring to?" Lisa asked but answered her questioned.

"Be ready? Be ready for what?" Steve also asked.

Raquel knelt beside the chest with no hesitation and looked at her siblings. "What do you think is inside? More artifacts? A clue to how the Smithsonian got a fake?"

"Raquel, we do not know, and I am sure the Smithsonian does not know, so someone needs to open the darn chest and see what is in it," David firmly said. "Maybe Betancourt can do it," he softly added.

Pedro gestured to them. "Perhaps it's best if all of you open it. I believe the compass chose you, not Señor Betancourt."

"Wait," Andrea states, handing the compass to Betancourt. The moment the compass was in his hands, the faint glow stops.

"It is not my destiny, Morales. It is yours," he said and handed the compass back to Andrea. The faint glow started up again.

Turning to Raquel, Andrea said. "You do it, Raquel." "Me? Why not you or David?"

"Señorita, you are the eldest," Pedro said. "In Taíno culture and tradition, the eldest bears the greatest responsibility."

With a deep breath, Raquel reached for the chest. Her fingers brushed the latch, and a faint hum filled the air. The Gran Cemi glowed brighter, its light pulsing as if in response.

"Wait," Andrea said, grabbing her arm. "Shouldn't we think this through? What if it's a trap?"

Raquel looked at her siblings, then at Pedro, who nodded in quiet encouragement while Betancourt just stood there just studying the situation.

She exhaled and lifted the lid.

Chapter 29

Treasure

Looking inside the small chest Raquel found a collection of photographs, letters, and small keepsakes. The items were meticulously arranged and well preserved. Raquel picked up a photograph from the top of the pile.

"Will you look at that," Andrea said. "That's... that's Abuela and Abuelo!"

Raquel held the faded photograph up to the glowing light of her torch. Sure enough, it was a picture of their grandparents, young and beaming, standing in front of a rectangular house. You could see in the background, the silhouette of the same mountain range where they now stood could be seen.

David groaned. "You've got to be kidding me. A photo of our grandparents! We came all this way, through caves and glowing compasses, for a family photo album?"

Raquel noticed an envelope that simply said, "To my beloved grandchildren". She recognised her grandfather's handwriting. She opened it carefully, her hands trembling, and began to read aloud:

"To my beloved grandchildren,

If you are reading this, then the compass has guided you here, as it was meant to. You are part of something greater than treasure or material wealth. The Gran Cemi and the compass are reminders of our heritage, of where we come from. But the greatest treasure of all is not gold or artifacts; it is the bond of family and the truth of who you are.

The keepsakes in this chest are pieces of our history. They hold stories of love, sacrifice, and resilience. Take them with you. Honour them. And above all, stay connected to one another, for that bond is your greatest strength."

Raquel's voice cracked as she finished the letter. The siblings stood in silence for a moment, the weight of their abuelo's words sinking in.

Andrea reached for a small silver locket in the chest and opened it. Inside was a picture of a younger Francisco holding their father as a baby. "This must be dad when he was a baby," she said showing the locket to her siblings, "he must have left this for us," she whispered.

David crossed his arms and huffed. "So, no treasure. No gold, silver, jewels. Nothing. Just... family history. I mean, it's sweet and all, but after everything we've been through, I was kind of expecting, I don't know, more, at least a pile of gold coins or rubies, something."

Raquel smirked. "Oh, come on, David. You don't seriously think every cave leads to treasure chests full of jewels, do you?"

"Yeah," Andrea chimed in. "What were you expecting?"

"I do not know but I was hoping for something that's for sure," David remarked.

Raquel took a moment and walked around the grand chamber. She stopped and turned to her siblings. "David, Andrea, do you realise what this means?"

Both siblings looking confused and shook their heads.

"It means our grandparents are descendants from the Taino people, so is our father and thus we carry some Taino blood in us!"

Pedro stepping forward. "Perhaps your treasure is in the chest you found. That knowledge is worth more than gold, no?"

"Just what I need right now. Philosophy or a corny quip. Just what I need right now and spoken by a man who appears to have no bills to pay."

Pedro smiled and nodded to the affirmative.

The siblings burst into laughter, their earlier tension melting away. Even David couldn't keep his grumpy facade, finally breaking into a grin.

As they packed the chest and prepared to leave, the compass dimmed, its purpose fulfilled. The Gran Cemi glowed faintly, almost as if bidding them farewell, as did the compass in Andrea's hand. For the first time in years, the siblings felt truly connected. Not just to each other, but to their roots.

David heaved the little chest onto his shoulder and groaned, pretending it was heavy. "Okay, fine. Maybe this family bond thing is worth something. But next time, let's find an adventure with actual treasure."

Raquel nudged him playfully. "Who says this wasn't treasure, David?"

He rolled his eyes but smiled. "Fine. But I'm calling dibs on the next glowing compass."

As they departed the chamber, Pedro smiled, knowing he and Pablo would return soon to continue attending to the Gran Cemi of Patina.

Chapter 30

Secrets

As the siblings began their descent from the mountains, they realised that this adventure had been unexpected in so many ways. It brought them closer than ever.

Raquel carried the small chest carefully. David, in deep thought about his newfound treasure and Andrea held the compass in her hand, acting like, well, just a compass, emitting no glow as it did before, a sign that its purpose had been fulfilled.

Pedro and Pablo walked alongside them, sharing stories of the Taíno people and the legends of the Gran Cemi. As they reached the base of the mountain trail, Raquel turned to them.

"Pedro, Pablo," Raquel said, "Thank you so much for everything you both did for us. We couldn't have done this without you, and we will be forever grateful."

Pedro nodded. "It was our honour to guide you. Your family's history is intertwined with this land, and we hope this journey brought you closer to it."

"It did," Andrea said with a big smile.

As they shook hands goodbye, Pablo mentioned, "Betancourt says he'll be heading to Santiago de Cuba to do some digging into these legends. He'll be in touch with you, I'm sure."

"We'll look forward to it," David said. "Hoping he finds gold treasure and calls for help."

With that statement, they all broke out laughing as they parted ways. The siblings made their way back to La Habana, where they spent their last days in Cuba reflecting on everything they'd learned. They visited the house where their grandparents and parents had lived, and they had grown up. They even had a chance to visit the cemetery where their grandparents rested.

The night before departing, they stood on the Malecón at sunset, looking out into the ocean.

"It's strange," Andrea remarked. "I always thought of Miami as home. But being here, it feels like we're part of something bigger."

Raquel nodded. "This trip reminded us of where we come from, and how much of who we are is because of our roots."

David grinned. "I guess we should've listened to Abuela when she used to tell those stories, huh?"

"Better late than never," Andrea teased.

The flight back to Miami was uneventful. Camila and Julio welcomed their children, and Raquel immediately took out the small chest and shared the keepsakes and Francisco's letter with their parents.

Julio's eyes filled with tears as he saw the photographs and read his father's message, a moment of healing and connection that brought the entire family closer.

Francisco's final request had been completed.

Meanwhile, back in the mountains, Pedro and Pablo stood in front of the Gran Cimi de Patana. Pedro ran his hand over the carved symbols on the walls, murmuring a prayer in the ancient Taíno tongue.

Pedro softly said to his cousin, "The Morales have found their answers."

Pablo responded: "And now, we must go on guarding ours."

The two men began moving large, moss-covered stones that had been stacked against the far wall. It was backbreaking work, hard work, but they had committed to this many years ago and they knew the significance of what lay hidden.

As the last rock was removed, the light from their lanterns illuminated the treasure. Silver, jewels, and gold, glittering in the light. These were relics of the Taíno people, gifts passed down by their ancestors to safeguard.

Pablo stepped back and spoke to his cousin: "The great god that descended from the heavens... Our ancestors said he would return one day. Pedro, you and I are to protect these until that time."

Pedro nodded solemnly. "This is our legacy, just as the chest was theirs. We will do our part."

After they both shared another prayer, they carefully re-concealed the treasure. They walked back to the small entrance to the chamber and Pedro extinguished the lantern.

The secrets of the Taíno would remain safe for now.

When the god from the shinning ship returned to reclaim them, Pedro and Pablo hoped to still be alive to receive them. If not, they now knew where three Taínos lived in America.

And so, the mountain would continue to keep its Taíno mysteries, its treasures, just as it had for centuries.

About The Author
José F. Nodar

Flung into one of life's most daunting challenges at just eleven years old, José's journey began in Havana, Cuba. The Cuban Revolution uprooted his family, forcing his parents to make a heart-wrenching decision: send him away alone to safety. José boarded a plane, uncertain of what lay ahead, and landed not in the comfort of familiar faces but at an orphanage in a small Georgia town called Washington.

For the next seven years, he navigated life as a stranger in a foreign land. Letters were few, and the hope of reuniting with his parents became a distant dream. Finally, at eighteen—now a high school graduate in Atlanta—he embraced his family once again. The reunion was bittersweet for José had grown up without them, becoming independent far sooner than most.

Determined to carve out a life for himself, José pursued a degree in Business Administration at Georgia State University. He stepped into the world of finance, starting at First National Bank of Atlanta (now Wells Fargo). His natural talent for numbers and strategic thinking propelled him to become a project manager in financial consulting, leading high stakes ventures. His career took him across the globe, from bustling cities in the United States to financial hubs in Europe and even the sunburnt coasts of Australia.

It was in Camden, New South Wales, that a new chapter of José's life began. While exploring the quiet rhythms of this Australian town, José stumbled upon a local writers' group. What began as a casual interest soon grew into an unquenchable passion. The stories swirling in his mind took shape, and from that creative spark, Danny Monk, his first major character, was born—a mischievous, intriguing figure who captured the complexities José had observed throughout his life. Writing Danny's story was a revelation, and with that, José discovered a new calling.

Fast forward to today. José is not just a writer but a prolific storyteller, balancing multiple projects at once. He is deep into his seventh short story collection while simultaneously crafting his latest work—a crime novel slated for release in 2026. His books, filled with engaging characters and complex narratives, reflect a life rich with experiences, challenges, and triumphs.

Yet José's world is not confined to the keyboard and screen. Inspiration comes from everywhere, and one of his favourite pastimes is to wander the local mall, quietly observing people, noting quirks, behaviours, and snippets of conversation that might spark a new character or plot twist. When he's not writing or gathering ideas, José immerses himself in literature, feeding his mind with the words of others.

Outside of his creative pursuits, José treasures the simple pleasures of life—particularly long walks with his wife, Miriam, through the scenic streets of Spring Farm. Their leisurely strolls are a cherished routine, moments of reflection where stories, memories, and dreams intertwine.

José's life is a tapestry woven from adversity, perseverance, and creativity. From the orphanage in Georgia to the financial districts of the world, and now to the quiet corners of Spring Farm, where stories are born, his journey is a testament to the resilience of the human spirit. And with each book he writes, José not only tells stories but also leaves behind pieces of himself, enriching the lives of readers across the globe.

Of course, your comments, and reviews are always welcome.

Please be sure you visit my website https://worldbookreviews.com.au/book-reviews/ and let me know what you thought of this novel and any of my books.

Good, bad, or indifferent, I welcome your honest opinion.

Thank you for your purchase!

José F. Nodar © 2025

Other books by José F. Nodar

English

- Books, Pens & Larceny
- Mending Hearts at Crystal Cove
- A Love Finally Spoken
- The Ghost Detective's First Case
- The Legacy Compass
- The Universe Between Us
- The Time Bus
- SEX
- Stories to Share with My Partner Book 1
- Stories to Share with My Partner Book 2
- Stories to Share with My Partner Book 3
- Stories to Share with My Partner Book 4
- Stories to Share with My Partner Book 5
- Stories to Share with My Partner Book 6
- Stories to Share with My Partner Book 7

Other books by José F. Nodar

Spanish

- Cuentos Para Compartir con Mi Pareja Libro 1
- Cuentos Para Compartir con Mi Pareja Libro 2
- Cuentos Para Compartir con Mi Pareja Libro 3
- Libros, Bolígrafos y Hurto
- Reparando Corazones en Crystal Cove
- Un Amor Expresado
- El Autobús del Tiempo

www.ingramcontent.com/pod-product-compliance
Lightning Source LLC
Chambersburg PA
CBHW061728070526
44583CB00024B/3052